EVERY CLICHÉ
IN THE BOOK

Also by Peggy Rosenthal

Words and Values: Some Leading Words and Where They Lead Us
(Oxford University Press, 1984)

EVERY CLICHÉ IN THE BOOK

Peggy Rosenthal and George Dardess

Illustrations by Peter LaVigna
Concepts for illustrations by The CRAG

QUILL

WILLIAM MORROW
NEW YORK

Library of Congress Cataloging-in-Publication Data

Rosenthal, Peggy.
   Every cliché in the book.

   Summary: Presents well-known clichés under the
headings: sentiments, situations, sources, and sounds.
   1. English language—Terms and phrases. 2. English
language—Style. [1. English language—Terms and
phrases. 2. English language—Idioms] I. Dardess,
George. II. LaVigna, Peter, ill. III. Title.
PE1442.R6   1988   428   87-36032
ISBN 0-688-06114-1 (pbk.)

Printed in the United States of America

First Quill Edition

1 2 3 4 5 6 7 8 9 10

BOOK DESIGN BY BETH TONDREAU

Preface

Scene: Late on a warm autumn afternoon, just after the conclusion of Ms. Goldpaper's class in English 10. Chalk dust hangs in the air. All students have left except for Ed Earnest, who has stayed to ask Ms. Goldpaper about the C he has received on his paper, "New Light Shed on Shakespeare."

MS. G. (wearily but kindly): Hi, Ed. What can I do for you? You look as if you have a question.

ED: Well, yes, I do, Ms. Goldpaper. I—I just don't know why I got a C on my paper. It sounds good to me, and it doesn't have a single comma splice!

MS. G.: C stands for "clichéd," Ed. You've got every cliché in the book in there. Haven't I told you to avoid clichés like the plague? Remember, they're the product of a lazy mind! They're dull, trite, weak, outworn . . .

. . . hackneyed, overworked, dead on their feet, good for nothing but the garbage bin, not worth the paper they're printed on . . . yes, yes, yes. We all know the standard criticisms of clichés. In fact, these put-downs of clichés are themselves clichés. And like many other clichés, they do have some truth in them: Ms. Goldpaper and her fellow teachers are right to condemn clichés as a bad influence on our minds when we want to be original or reflective. But apart from the occasions (actually rare) when originality and reflection are called for, clichés aren't all that bad.

The purpose of this book is to give clichés a chance to show off their good side. Clichés play a lot of positive roles in our culture. They act as a common social bond; they pass on the insights of the ages; they entertain us with snappy wit. Yes, in a sense they're guilty, as accused, of being dead metaphors; but in another sense their images are full of life. Yes, they're overworked; yet they never tire of coming to our aid when nothing else could serve us quite so well. The product of a lazy mind? Yes, in certain individual usages. But taken all together they're the product of a mind that's energetic, inventive, creative: the collective mind of our cultural consciousness.

The book's structure is designed to offer clichés a stage for performing their positive functions. Section I presents clichés expressing our common moods, attitudes, and judgments. Section II is a series of scenes where clichés serve us in familiar social situations. In Section III, the spotlight is on the visual richness of clichés, which are presented according to the images they contain. In Section IV, clichés sing for their supper; their rhythm and rhyme and other special sound effects take the stage.

An example will clarify this structural design and will also show how a single cliché can perform multiple functions and so make its appearance in several places in the book. "His sun has set": This is a judgment about someone, so it appears in Section I with clichés describing personalities. To bolster someone's confidence, we might say, "Your sun hasn't set," which therefore turns up in the "Bolstering" scene of Section II. The image of "sun" puts this cliché in the "Air" part of Section III. And the alliteration of "sun has set" puts it in the list of alliterative clichés in Section IV.

Not every cliché fits into so many categories. "If you can't say something nice, don't say anything at all" appears only in Section II, in the monologue of "Parents to Kids." "Can't see the forest for the trees" appears only in Section III, with clichés whose metaphors are plants and vegetables. "I'll tear my hair out" turns up twice: in Section I, with clichés expressing anger; and in Section III, with clichés containing body parts. "Proud as a peacock" makes three appearances: as a personality description in Section I; with animal images in Section III; and in the alliterative list in Section IV. If you want to find a particular cliché quickly, turn to the index, where all the clichés in the book are listed alphabetically.

The variety of rhetorical riches that clichés display, and of functions they perform, calls for an assortment of modes of presentation; so the book is like a variety show. The most frequent mode of presentation is the list: lists of clichés arranged so as to bring forward some common feature. Short dramatic scripts play with clichés in particular situations. Brief essays, called "Food for Thought," offer an occasional change of pace, an idea to chew on or mull over. And providing continuity throughout, as well as illustrating the comic nature of clichés, are the cartoons. A main cartoon character will act as our master of ceremonies, so he needs now to be introduced: He's Buddy McCliche, who will take us through every cliché in the book.

Peggy Rosenthal
George Dardess
November 1986

Acknowledgments

Since the purpose of this book is to celebrate clichés as a product of our collective imagination, it's appropriate that gathering them was truly a collective project. Friends and relatives of all ages contributed—sometimes, maybe, against their wishes. One of our collection methods was to ask people to speak to us only in clichés, while we recorded them on slips of paper we carried in our pockets and kept on every table in the house. This procedure naturally made normal conversation difficult, and we'd like to thank everyone who put up with us for the two years we were compiling the book.

Special thanks go to a few people who showed special perseverance. To Helene and Bob Atwan, who brainstormed most of the Personality clichés with us during a dinner out, and to the waitress who kept supplying cocktail napkins for us to write them on. To our parents, who let our vacations together become cliché-collecting expeditions: Peg's Dad provided us with over a hundred Body clichés one afternoon on the beach, no doubt under the inspiration of all the exposed body parts. To our son, Eric, and his friends, who survived the confusing experience of being told by teachers to clear their heads of clichés while being urged by parents to fill their heads full of them. To Mary Mickle, our country cousin who spun out Plant and Animal clichés with us during an afternoon drive. To Susie and Kent Winchester, who did some expert cliché-collecting in the wilds of the suburbs. To Holly and Mike Kane, who win the prize for mailing in the most clichés; they sent us literally boxloads. Finally, special thanks to our agent, John Wright, who set the wheels in motion by coming up with the original concept for the book, and who remained a friend to the end.

Contents

Introducing Buddy McCliche

Gosh! What a picture-
perfect day this is! Just
the moment for a stroll
into the great outdoors.
A day like this
gives you a
new lease
on life!
Puts a smile on
your face and a
song in your heart!

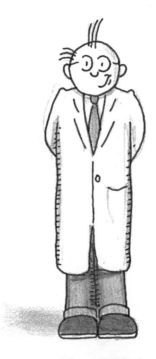

Buddy McCliche

Uh-oh! Maybe I spoke
too soon! That must be my
old pal, Gloomy Gus,
I s'pose I oughta see
if I can pull him
out of it.

Down in the dumps

Hey, Gus! Come off it!
Get rid of that long
face! You look like
you lost your last
friend!

It's no use, Buddy McCliche—I
can't go on—I'm
all messed up—
I've had it.

Something the cat dragged in

Aw c'mon, Gus—Don't sell yourself short! You're not dead yet. Life can't always be a bowl of cherries. Look for that old silver lining!

Had it up to here

Yeah? I dunno—life's been a real downer.

Say hey! Look at the bird up there singing for pure joy.

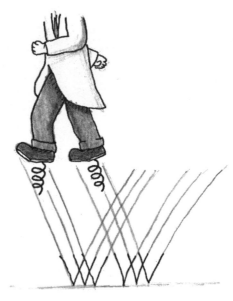

Put a spring in your step

Gus, for crying out loud—

Don't stew in your own juices

Maybe, but I kinda got to like it down here.

Yeah—
if only
I could
get this
load off
my mind!
Then I
could
really
hear
it!

Get this load off my mind

Merciful heavens, Gus—no
wonder you've been so
weighed down! You'll
be walking on air
after this!

On cloud nine

Wow! I feel like a million bucks! And it's all 'cause of you, Buddy McCliche. You're the best friend a Gloomy Gus like me ever had!

Tut, it was nothing, really.

We have to stick together

SECTION ONE
SENTIMENTS

FOOD FOR THOUGHT #1: "YOU'VE GOTTA BEGIN SOMEWHERE"

There's something of the Buddy McCliche in all of us. And it's a good thing there is. Clichés are a common cultural bond; if you don't know them, aren't comfortable with them, you're alienated from your society.

More about how and why clichés act as a common bond of our culture will become apparent as the book goes along. For a start, this opening section, "Sentiments," presents clichés that express common moods, attitudes, judgments, perceptions. The first group, entitled "In Touch with One's Feelings," contains things we say about ourselves; the clichés that come next, in "Personalities," are things we say about others. In both categories, there's often exaggeration. That's the comic element of clichés: We almost never feel *this* bad (or good) or think someone else is *that* awful (or great).

Yet there's a psychological validity to many of the clichés. They do express well the particular personality type or mood; that's why they've become clichés. When we're feeling low, for instance, we do feel "down in the dumps," as if we've "hit rock bottom." And when we're angry, we do feel as if we're "blowing up" or "hitting the roof."

At such moments there's personal satisfaction in having at our fingertips a stock of phrases that express just how we feel. And the fact that it's a *common* stock makes communication about our moods clear. If a friend calls you and says, "I'm not myself today, I'm at loose ends, I'm coming apart at the seams," you know to rush right over and give her a helping hand. If a colleague at work comes at you with, "I'll stop at nothing, I'm dead set on it," you know not to stand in her way.

In Touch with One's Feelings

In touch with one's feelings

ANGER

It makes me see red
  makes my blood boil
  makes me burn
  burns me up
  makes me sick

I'm ready to have a fit
       raise Cain
       tear my hair out
       flip my lid
       blow up
       hit the ceiling

Blow his stack

It drives me batty
       nuts
       wild
       haywire
       up a wall
       up a tree
       out of my mind

It sets my teeth on edge
  gets my dander up

It gets on my nerves

It gets my goat

I'm at the end of my rope
   at my wit's end
   fit to be tied
   fed up

I've had it up to here

It gets my goat

FATE

I'm putting the best face on it
   keeping a stiff upper lip
   smiling through my tears
   taking it in stride
   taking it with a grain of salt
   counting my blessings
   biting the bullet
   rolling with the punches
   flowing with the tide
   letting bygones be bygones
   letting sleeping dogs lie
   making the most of it
   weathering the storm

I'm at peace with the world

It's a labor of love
    a saving grace
    my cross to bear
    all in a day's work
    all the same to me
    not in the cards
    not the end of the world
    never too late
    just the luck of the draw
    just one of those things
    just part of the give-and-take
    just water over the dam

A blessing in disguise

No use crying over spilt milk

    That's how the cookie crumbles

        Let the chips fall where they may

            I may as well be hanged for a sheep as for a lamb

                Oh, well, live and learn

So it goes

It comes with the territory

It won't hurt to try

There's always a bright side

It could be worse

That's life

LOWS

It's all downhill from here

I'm feeling down
    run down
    down and out
    down in the dumps

In the pits

Things are going from bad to worse

I'm leading a dog's life
    wearing myself out
    wearing myself ragged
    crying my eyes out

crying my heart out
feeling like dirt

I'm in the depths of despair
   at a dead end
   half dead
   dead tired
   under the weather
   sick at heart
   limp as a dishrag
   all washed up
   too pooped to pop

Not up to snuff

It's taken the wind out of my sails
   left me drained
   coming down around my ears

I've struck out
   fallen on evil times
   got the rainy-day blues
   got a sinking feeling
   hit rock bottom
   hit the skids

It's the beginning of the end
   a lost cause
   all over

I throw in the towel

There's no end in sight

HIGHS

I'm as high as a kite
    in seventh heaven
    on cloud nine
    riding high
    walking on air
    sitting on top of the world
    sitting pretty
    basking in the glow

                Everything's coming up roses

                The world is my oyster

                It's my moment in the sun
                    a shot in the arm
                    tip-top

I'm tickled to death
    tickled pink
    pleased as punch
    laughing my head off
    kicking up my heels
    going great guns
    going all out

I'm acting like there's no tomorrow
like it's going out of style

I feel like a million bucks

A million bucks

I'm having a ball
feeling my oats

I'm on a roll
up for it

Things are looking up

CONFUSION

I'm beside myself
    losing my mind

I'm not myself today

I'm at sea
    in the dark

I'm going in circles
    going crazy
    going bananas

In limbo

I'm beating my head against a wall
    climbing the walls

I'm coming apart at the seams
    at loose ends

                    I'm at sixes and sevens

                    I'm of two minds about it

                    I don't know whether to laugh or cry

RESOLUTION

I'm dead set on it

I'll jump in with both feet
    bend over backward
    roll up my sleeves and get to work
    take matters into my own hands
    take the bull by the horns
    leave no stone unturned
    get to the bottom of this
    stake my life on it
    stop at nothing

Pull out all the stops

by hook or by crook

at all costs

once and for all

till hell freezes over
till the cows come home

I'm dead set against it

I'm putting my foot down
    standing my ground
    sticking to my guns
    throwing up my hands
    washing my hands of the whole matter

I'm digging in my heels

I wouldn't touch it with a ten-foot pole

I'll leave 'em in the dust
              wondering what hit 'em

I'll show 'em a thing or two
              who's boss
              what I'm made of
              who's running this show

I'll give 'em what for

Wild horses couldn't make me

I'll eat my hat if I do

Enough is enough

That's the last straw

Over my dead body

Personalities

Hi, Toots! Let me introduce you
Did you just blow into town?

I've got more friends than you can shake a stick at. He's Steady
Eddy.

He's . . .
   down to earth
   the salt of the earth
   cool, calm, and collected
   an everyday guy
   a meat-and-potatoes guy
   a good egg
   a straight arrow
   on an even keel

A pillar of the community

He's the backbone of society

He has a good head on his shoulders
    has his feet on the ground
    holds his own
    stands on his own two feet

That Steady Ed is a real peach! Trouble is, he's a bit too
foursquare. My next friend is a tad more lively.

He's a Loonybird but he's a live wire.

Fills the bill

You see, he's . . .

off his rocker
off the wall
out to lunch
out of his mind
out in left field

Crazy as a loon

nutty as a fruitcake
one for the books
stark raving mad

Ready for the loony bin

He flipped his lid
     lost his marbles
         went off the deep end
         went haywire

He's got a screw loose somewhere
        tilting at windmills

He oughta have his head examined

Lock him up and throw away the key! Keep your distance from *him.* Hook up with those two characters over there.

It's Honest Abe

He's . . .

>   a man of his word
>   true to his word

He speaks his mind
>   says it like it is
>   calls a spade a spade
>   has the courage of his convictions
>   shoots from the hip
>   lays it on the line

He doesn't mince words

He'll level with you
He's on the up-and-up

While Two-faced over there . . .
    lies through his teeth
    hits below the belt
    looks like butter wouldn't melt in his mouth

A master of deception

He's a real snake in the grass
I wouldn't trust him as far as I could throw him

        She looks like a good catch!
        Why don't you give her a whirl? She's a real go-getter.

She . . .
    goes all out
    gives it all she's got
    gives it one hundred percent
    sets her sights high
    burns the midnight oil
    doesn't let the grass grow under her feet

She has a lot of irons in the fire

She's always on the go
        at the cutting edge

She can write her own ticket

She's a dynamo
        a ball of fire
        a real eager beaver

While this other guy, the Wimp, is . . .
                        as quiet as a mouse

He doesn't come out of his shell
        hides his head in the sand
        hides his light under a bushel

He hides his head in the sand

He'll never set the world on fire

He's afraid of his own shadow
always on the sidelines
tied to his mother's apron strings
the stay-at-home type
a clinging vine
a wet blanket
got nothing going for him

He'll never amount to anything

He's a loser, but Joe Cool looks like a winner.

He's . . .
the life of the party
dressed to the nines
all decked out
a ladies' man
tall, dark, and handsome
sowing his wild oats

He sweeps them off their feet

He has an eye for the ladies

While that guy with the Short-Fuse . . .
    blows hot and cold

He gets carried away
Making mountains out of molehills

He's got a pet peeve

He always has a bone to pick
    goes off half-cocked
    flies off the handle

My other friend's a sharpie. She's . . .
                      sharp as a tack
                      on the ball
                      in the know

She knows the ropes
    knows which side her bread is buttered on
    doesn't turn a hair
    doesn't miss a trick
    has a bagful of tricks
    has a magic touch
    plays her cards close to her chest

While that Dumb Bunny . . .
    doesn't have a clue

She knows all the angles

He doesn't play with a full deck

He's three bricks short of a full load
    rowing a boat with one oar in the water

He doesn't have much upstairs
His elevator doesn't go to the top floor
He was behind the door when the brains were passed out
     (The lights are on, but nobody's home)
He's not all there
    slower than molasses
    dumb as an ox

This place is a zoo.

That gal's a Snob. She thinks she's the cat's meow.

She's . . .
    proud as a peacock

Strutting her stuff

But she's just a big fish in a small pond
    too big for her breeches
    a stuffed shirt
    too full of herself

She has a swelled head
    looks down her nose at the world
    thinks she's hot stuff
        God's gift to the world
    acts like she was born with a silver spoon in her mouth

While none of this gets his goat because that guy's a saint

He's . . .
    as gentle as a lamb
    wouldn't hurt a fly
    has a heart of gold

                His heart's in the right place
                He'll lend a helping hand
                    give you the shirt off his back

He goes out of his way
    goes the extra mile
    goes to extra lengths

                He's as good as gold

This place is a gold mine. You can't go wrong.

That's because variety is the spice of life! And you haven't seen
the half of it yet. It takes *all* kinds to make the world go 'round.

The Individualist. She's . . .
                one of a kind

A lone wolf

        one in a million
        her own person
        a breed apart

She has a mind of her own
She's in a class by herself
She'll break out of the pack
      break out of the mold
She marches to the beat of a different drummer

        And here we've got . . .
           a stubborn one.
           He's stubborn as a mule
           He can't change his spots
           He's a tough nut to crack

        He takes the bit between his teeth
           won't budge an inch
           is set in his ways

Talking to him is like talking to the wall

He's a Take-Charge-Guy
He's . . .
    at the helm
    in the driver's seat
He doesn't take a backseat to anybody
He's king of the hill
He's cock of the walk
He has the world in the palm of his hand

He rules the roost

He's a Has-Been. He's . . .
        all washed up
        over the hill
        ready to be put out to pasture

His star is on the wane

His sun has set

The Brain. He's . . .
                smart as a whip
                a walking encyclopedia
He has a memory like an elephant
    is a gold mine of information

The Dreamer. He . . .
                has his head in the clouds
                builds castles in the air
                doesn't see beyond his nose
                lives in a world of his own

The Boor. He . . .
                comes on strong
                comes on like gangbusters
                throws his weight around

Swears like a trooper

always has to have the last word
toots his own horn
doesn't let himself get pushed around

Scrooge. He's . . .
a penny-pincher
hard-hearted
hard as nails

A slave driver

He has a mean streak
        a heart of stone
He makes money hand over fist

        The Busybody. She . . .
                        tells tales out of school
                        talks a blue streak
                        can talk your ear off
                        gives you an earful
                        has the gift of gab
                        has a finger in every pie

The Optimist. She . . .
            makes the most of it
            sees the bright side of things
            is happy as a lark
            hasn't a care in the world
            looks through rose-colored glasses

        The Oaf. He . . .
                        has two left feet
        He's all thumbs
            like a bull in a china shop

Deeper Meanings

FOOD FOR THOUGHT #2: "PLUMBING THE DEPTHS"

Many clichés probe life's deeper meanings. They take its measure; they evaluate and pass judgment; they give us what we take as words of wisdom. Following are three groups of such words: In "Just for Good Measure," clichés that imply or set standards; in "Thinking It Through," clichés that try to describe how our minds work; in "The Meaning of Life," clichés that offer answers to some of the perennial human questions.

Clichés convey our culture's sense of meaning through a variety of images, but two seem especially popular: cards (the game of life) and pathways (the road of life). No doubt it's their symbolic richness that makes these two images favorites. "A wild card," "the luck of the draw," "it's not in the cards," all capture our sense of life as random, arbitrary, out of our control. But, as if to balance this fatalism, clichés such as "a few years down the road," "I'm with you every step of the way,"—even "I've run into a roadblock" or "gone up a blind alley"—capture our equally strong sense of possibility, choice, and purpose, our sense that there is indeed a direction to human life.

Gone up a blind alley

JUST FOR GOOD MEASURE

Clichés having to do with measuring are grouped here according
to their common terms: words such as *weight, inch, long, far,*
and *more.* Together, these clichés give a hint of how often
we take the measure of a situation, whatever that situation
might be.

The Long   and the Short of It

long time no see   cut it short
in for the long haul   make short work of it
a long row to hoe   come up short
in the long run   sell him short
a long way to go   give him short shrift
a little goes a long way   get the short end of the stick
we've come a long way   short and sweet
not by a long shot

That's about the size of it

Watch Your Weight

weigh your words
pull your weight
throw your weight around
you're worth your weight in gold

A dead weight

So Near . . .

near and dear

. . . and Yet So Far

far and wide
few and far between
go so far as to say
as far as that goes
don't go too far

Give Her an Inch . . .

She won't budge an inch
She's within an inch of her life

. . . and She'll Take a Mile

She goes the extra mile
    went a mile a minute
    missed it by a mile

For Better . . .

Better late than never

. . . or Worse

It could be worse
A fate worse than death

The More the Merrier

Get more than you bargained for
More than you can shake a stick at
More than meets the eye
Does more harm than good

There's a lot more where these came from

THINKING IT THROUGH

Here is a series of clichés dramatizing a familiar situation: the private struggle to think through a problem, get an idea, figure something out. Arranged in order of the stereotypical stages of the thinking process, these clichés are interesting both for their abundance and for the variety of their images. The abundance suggests how much we pay attention to our mind, to thought itself; the variety suggests how little we know about what thought really is. In our effort to understand the mysterious mental process, we often imagine it going on in our bodies (we "get our teeth into" a problem or "put our finger on it"). In our attempt to picture an idea, which is by nature abstract, we make it comfortably concrete: We "bounce it around" (like a ball) or "mull it over" (like a brew). Sometimes we even get violent in our eagerness to "get a grip on" our thoughts about thought: We "attack a problem" or "tackle" it; the solution "jumps out at us" or "hits us like a ton of bricks."

When you stop and think about it . . .
    Off the top of my head
    It crossed my mind

It boggles my mind
It's all up in the air
It doesn't hold water
I don't have the foggiest idea
I'm just beating around the bush
I'm grasping at straws
I'm splitting hairs
I'm racking my brains

Just a shot in the dark

I can't make heads or tails of it
It's back to the drawing board

Drawing a blank

I'm going in circles
    jumping to conclusions
    taking it too far
    off the track
    up a blind alley

It's a real can of worms

It's on the tip of my tongue
I can't put my finger on it

I haven't scratched the surface
I'll have to start from scratch
I've got my work cut out for me

On second thought . . .

I'll put on my thinking cap
    put first things first

I'll bounce some ideas around
    boil them down
    mull them over
    let them sink in

I'll get down to brass tacks
    pinpoint the problem
    attack it head on
    tackle it
    stand it on its head
    get my teeth into it
    chew it over

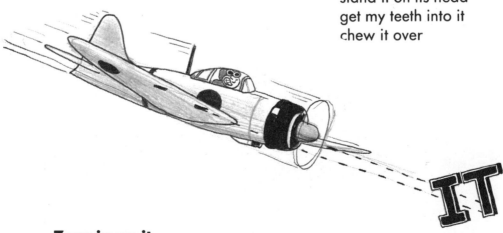

Zero in on it

The idea jumped out at me

It hit me like a ton of bricks

It's all falling into place

I think I'm on to something

I think I've come up with it

Now I've got a handle on it

It's a turning point

I've nailed it down

It dawned on me

I saw the light

It rings a bell

It's fresh in my mind
    as clear as day
    crystal clear

A stroke of genius!

Right on target!

I've hit the nail on the head

      and

laid it to rest

THE MEANING OF LIFE

(In the 1930s and '40s, Americans were treated to a delightful character named Mr. Arbuthnot, the Cliché Expert, who was the creation of writer Frank Sullivan. Respectfully trying to imitate Sullivan's style, we do our best here to bring Mr. Arbuthnot back to life—in hopes that a glimpse of his ghost will spur readers to seek out the original. The Cliché Expert's words of wisdom can be found in several Sullivan collections, including *A Pearl in Every Oyster* and *A Rock in Every Snowball*).

"Mr. Arbuthnot on the Meaning of Life"

Q: Well, Mr. Arbuthnot, it's a great pleasure to speak to you again. You've been silent now for a long time—nearly forty years, if I remember correctly. Now, I'm sure our readers would like to know where you've been and what you've been thinking all that time.

A: Are you trying to say that you want me to fill you?

Q: "Fill you . . ."?

A: Fill you in, of course.

Q: Oh, right! How stupid of me!

A: Or bring you.

Q: Uh . . . how's that? "Bring you"?

A: Why, up to date!

Q: Goodness, how rusty I've gotten! I hope you won't take it—

A: To heart? Personally? Wrong?

Q: Well, ha ha, I've forgotten that one has to get up pretty early in the morning if he wants to keep up with you on clichés, Mr. Arbuthnot! You seem sharper now than . . . than . . .

A: Than what?

Q: Well, before . . . before what happened to you happened. Uh, by the way, what *did* happen to you since we last heard from you? Did you pass—

A: Exactly: on.

Q: On?

A: Away.

Q: Away?

A: Into the next world. Into the beyond. Into the hereafter. Into the great unknown. Into the great pie in the sky.

Q: You're . . . you're *dead,* in other words?

A: As a doornail.

Q: I see. Well, I hadn't expected this somehow, although, when you come to think of it—

A: We all have to.

Q: Think of it?

A: Go.

Q: Go?

A: Go sometime.

Q: Yes. Very good observation! How true! Tell me this, though— What is it that you *can't* do in such a situation?

A: Two things. Live forever.

Q: That's one. The second?

A: Take it with you.

Q: Got it. I couldn't agree more. Now, were you alone on your journey or did you have a companion?

A: Alone at first, but eventually I met someone.

Q: Who was that?

A: My Maker.

Q: You mean—?

A: The Man.

Q: Man? But I thought—

A: The Man Upstairs.

Q: Ah, yes, *that* man. But you see, as much as we'd like to hear more about that relationship, it's in the nature of clichés—as you well know—to impart practical advice about life. So perhaps you wouldn't mind telling us what you've learned from your experience. From your present perspective, then, what words of counsel do you have for us who still walk the earth? For instance, while here, what shouldn't we miss?

A: A trick, of course.

Q: *Never?*

A: Except when it's not in the cards.

Q: Where should we let the chips fall?

A: Where they may.

Q: When should we play our hardest?

A: When the chips are down.

Q: Should we reach for something special at such a time?

A: Our ace in the hole.

Q: What should our expression be throughout this time?

A: Poker-faced.

Q: In general, what kind of luck should we hope for?

A: The luck of the draw.

Q: Thank you, Mr. Arbuthnot. Life *is* like playing a game of cards. But we'd all like to know how many such games we can expect to win?

A: You can't expect to win them all.

Q: Can't you be more precise as to our probable wins and losses?

A: You win some and you lose some.

Q: I see. Well, that covers the idea pretty well, I think. Now, more to the point, exactly what sort of a thing is life?

A: A path, a passage, a road, a journey.

Q: And, again from your perspective, what particular task are we to perform at the end of this road?

A: Pushing up.

Q: Pushing up what?

A: Pushing up daisies.

Q: From where?

A: Six feet under.

Q: Doesn't sound so bad, I guess! Well, when are we going to get there?

A: A few years down the road.

Q: I mean, how *far* do we still have?

A: A long way to go.

Q: Are there dangers along the way?

A: There are tough times ahead.

Q: Will we run into anything?

A: Roadblocks, perhaps.

Q: Anything else?

A: Blind alleys.

Q: Goodness! This isn't the most cheery news. Can't you end on a happier note?

A: Yes, certainly—not on a note, however, but in a bowl.

Q: A bowl?

A: Of cherries. That's what life really *is,* you see. And the bowl really is cracked up.

Q: Cracked up?

A: Really is cracked up to what it's supposed to be.

Q: What's it all in? The bowl, I mean.

A: How you take it.

Q: How do *you* take it?

A: I don't take it. I look at it from the side.

Q: Which side?

A: The bright side, of course. I've got to get back now before they close.

Q: Before *what* closes?

A: The Gates.

Q: The *Pearly* Gates?—Oh Lord, Oh my God, he's beyond me. He's in another world. He up and left. So I guess that's all folks; our subject has escaped us. And, who knows? Maybe it was all over our heads in the first place.

FOOD FOR THOUGHT #3: "THERE'S NOTHING NEW UNDER THE SUN"

Is there really nothing new under the sun? Certain clichés do give that impression. They convey attitudes and insights that seem as old as the hills. "Too many cooks spoil the broth," "the apple doesn't fall far from the tree," "better safe than sorry"—lines like these have the ring of time-honored truth.

These clichés that express conventional wisdom might also be called proverbs. But exactly what sort of saying *should* be called a proverb is a question that scholars of the subject avoid. Though dictionaries try to pin the definition down to something like "a short, familiar statement of commonly accepted truth or judgment," the authoritative collections of proverbs insist on being much more inclusive. The *Oxford Dictionary of English Proverbs,* for instance, contains statements that are hardly familiar, such as "keep your breath to cool your broth," along with phrases that are hardly statements, such as "keeping the wolf from the door" or "a fine kettle of fish." These last two we would certainly call clichés.

Rather than fussing over definitions, then, it seems more fruitful just to acknowledge the popularity of philosophical-sounding sayings and to look briefly at the philosophy of life they convey. Some encourage a spirit of adventure:

> make hay while the sun shines
> you can't take it with you
> nothing ventured, nothing gained

But many more are cautionary:

> don't count your chickens before they're hatched
> don't change horses in mid stream
> don't upset the apple cart
> a stitch in time saves nine
> waste not, want not

An apple a day keeps the doctor away

This cautious, moderating note is struck, too, in the many lines that urge acceptance, resignation, tolerance:

> count your blessings
> every cloud has a silver lining
> beggars can't be choosers
> half a loaf is better than none

here today, gone tomorrow
tomorrow's another day
Rome wasn't built in a day
no pain, no gain
you win some, you lose some
you can't get blood out of a turnip
you can't have your cake and eat it too

Roll with the punches

don't make mountains out of molehills
don't cry over spilt milk
let bygones be bygones
boys will be boys
leave well enough alone
forgive and forget
live and let live
live and learn

Why, we might ask, is moderation the dominant tone of the domestic philosophy passed on in such commonplaces? And what purpose does this stock of commonplaces serve? The answer to both questions probably lies in the value that people seem to put on stability, on continuity, on common sense. The sense expressed in commonplaces is indeed common, and its very commonness gives it validity. What's common is communal: sense we can count on because it comes from collective human experience. And what's common is ordinary, familiar: sense we can fall back on, settle comfortably into—like the well-worn cushions of the family sofa—when life gets a bit rough or confusing. The common sense of conventional wisdom is reassuring because we know it's reliable. Like Rome, it wasn't built in a day. It has stood the test of time.

Admittedly we can also collapse into clichés, as into the sofa, out of sheer laziness. Those soft cushions might appeal to us because we're soft in the head. Such a suspicion is behind the typical derogatory descriptions of *cliché* and *commonplace* as "trite," "unoriginal," and "threadbare." (To call a saying a proverb is usually to praise it; to call it a cliché or a commonplace is usually to scorn it.)

Seeing commonplaces as positive, therefore, requires seeing originality as at least possibly negative, acknowledging that a conventional expression might carry more good sense than cleverness would. Although a sofa or a saying might be threadbare because we haven't bothered to replace it, it might be threadbare because it has served us so well over the years that nothing can take its (common) place.

SECTION TWO

SITUATIONS

FOOD FOR THOUGHT #4: "THERE'S A TIME AND A PLACE FOR EVERYTHING"

Certain situations seem to bring their own clichés along with them. It's easy to make fun of this, but there can be a positive social value to even the most mundane of human exchanges. We've all found ourselves, for instance, in utterly clichéd exchanges such as the following:

> ***A:*** Hi, how's the world treating you?
>
> ***B:*** Not bad. Can't complain. But I wish my kid would get his act together and stop letting life pass him by while he strums his guitar.
>
> ***A:*** Oh, he's a good kid. He'll shape up. At least he's not doing anything he shouldn't be doing. His heart's in the right place—but that's no surprise, he's a chip off the old block.
>
> ***B:*** Well, thanks, but it's time he learned a thing or two about the nuts and bolts of life. It's no picnic out there, you know. The kid doesn't have a glimmer that there are a whole bunch of people who'd just as soon eat you alive as look at you.

It's a dog eat dog world

A: Yep, kids today aren't what they used to be. They just want to hide their heads in the sand. But hang in there. Your kid'll come out of his shell. Kids just take longer to grow up these days. Well, so long, have a good one.

Out of context, this exchange sounds simply silly. But if A and B are neighbors who've had a tiff (maybe over the amp level of B's kid's "strumming"), then the availability of these clichéd lines helps them—yes—patch over their differences. If A has previously been going bongos because of that guitar but has now decided to try to "make the best of it," the clichés give her the medium to make that best: to express goodwill in common, noncontroversial lines that B will be grateful to be able to assent to. A's clichés about "kids" could even help ease the strain between B and his kid, by making his kid seem not abnormally lazy but just typical, normal, and therefore "not a bad kid after all."

In many other situations, too, clichés play a healing or bonding role. Because their terms *are* common to everyone in a culture, they can act as a common bond between people. Clichés can be a sort of social glue holding together people who would otherwise break apart into an uncommunicative alienation: strangers thrown together on airplanes or in long supermarket lines, fellow church members with strongly opposing political views, colleagues at work who drive each other wild, adults and teenagers, adults and their in-laws, middle-aged adults and slightly senile senior citizens.

It's true that clichés can be abusive instead of bonding; and among the "Situations" presented in this section, several include strings of clichés that either bring out the worst in us or articulate that "worst" that's already "out." We've all had the awful experience of feeling trapped in clichés during a quarrel. During a marital battle of words, for instance, we suddenly think, "Help, I'm in a soap opera! How can I get out?" That recognition itself—hearing that the lines we're hurling *are* clichés—is often enough to get us out.

A final positive note about clichés in social situations. Simply being able to utter appropriate clichés—being aware of the cliché that best fits the moment—can make people feel good about themselves. They feel good because the right cliché strikes, they know, a responsive chord in their listener. The two of them understand each other; they speak the same language; they're in harmony—both with each other and with the larger culture that is the prolific composer of their lines.

Quarreling and Making Up

A PLAY IN ONE ACT WITH A CONFLICT,
CRISIS, CLIMAX, AND HAPPY ENDING

Scene: A stereotypical suburban living room, containing stereotypical furnishings (TV, potted plants, etc.). Junior's new stereo is typically booming down from his bedroom. Little Sister is yakking on the phone. Snuffles, the golden retriever, is whining to be let out. Patches, the cat, is sharpening her claws on the edge of the sofa.

Characters: A stereotypical mom and pop, joined at the crisis by Buddy McCliche, who plays the role of Guardian Angel as well as adding a musical dimension to the proceedings.

Situation: For stereotypical reasons (the TV reception is bad, the hamburgers were overdone, the paperboy didn't deliver the paper, etc.), Mom and Pop are at

odds
sixes and sevens
loggerheads
each other's throats

In other words, they are

name calling
finding fault
lashing out
adding insult to injury
having a knock-down drag-out fight

Fighting tooth and nail

Mom: Stop treating me like dirt.

Pop: Oh, yeah? Well, two can play at that game, you know. I'm sick of being your doormat.

Mom: Oh, great! When it's *you* who's walking all over *me*!

Pop: Watch it, you're treading on thin ice!

Mom: And you're walking on eggshells.

Pop: Oh, is that so? Look who's got egg all over *her* face!

Mom: I never claimed to be a saint, did I?

Pop: And it's a darn good thing, too!

Mom: Oh, drop dead. The shoe fits the other foot, you know.

Pop: What's *that* supposed to mean?

Mom: Come off it. You know very well what I'm driving at.

Pop: Just what *are* you talking about?

Mom: Don't play innocent with me, Buster. It's as plain as the nose on your face.

Pop: Hey, what am I, a mind reader? Come clean, willya, for Pete's sake?

Mom: There you go calling me the scum of the earth again!

Pop: I did *not* say that.

Mom: Well, you *meant* it.

Pop: So what if I did?

Mom: That takes the cake! That's the last straw!

Pop: Pipe down for cripe sakes or you'll wake the dead.

Mom: You're not the man *I* married.

Pop: Oh? Who am I, then, someone else's husband? Then what does that make *you*?

Mom: How dare you! I've never been so insulted in all my life!

Pop: Aw, gimme a break. This is my reward for slaving at the salt mines and bringing home the bacon? You'd be out on the street in two seconds if I wasn't footing the bills.

Mom: That's a fine how-do-you-do after wasting the best years of my life working my fingers to the bone for you and your brats!

Pop: Now, wait just a second—

Mom: No, I won't, not until you tell me who died and made *you* king.

Pop: Get off my back, willya? And as for acting high and mighty—*you* should talk.

Mom: Takes one to know one!

Pop: Suit yourself. I've had it up to here.

At this point, Buddy McCliche is lowered by a wire from the ceiling. He is clothed in shining robes and wings. A blinking neon halo is fixed over his head. He sings the following hymn, accompanying himself on the ukulele, and returns to the upper regions once his message is given.)

Buddy McCliche (sings):

> Oh friends, since life's both nasty and short,
> It'll pay this quarrel to abort.
> Clichés have brought you to this fit
> (For that's the long and short of it);
> Clichés can you from it untangle—
> Clichés can end this hopeless wrangle.
> So patch your differences with glue
> Of words that meanness do eschew.
> Seek phrases calm and expressions mellow;
> Be kindly minded with your fellow.

Pop: Gee, I don't know how to say this, but . . .

Mom: Well?

Pop: I guess maybe . . . maybe I went too far.

Mom: Yeah, you blew it, all right.

Pop: True, I lost my head, but then it takes two to tango.

Mom: Mmm . . . You've got a point there, I suppose. I sort of fanned the flames.

Pop: Well, the other side of the coin is that at least we cleared the air a little.

Mom: Sometimes it's good to let it all hang out.

Pop: That's right. People go nuts when they can't let off a little steam now and then.

Mom: Exactly. You can go batty if you don't confront your feelings from time to time.

Pop: It kinda gives you a new lease on life.

Mom: It puts things in their place.

Pop: It gives you a proper perspective.

Mom: A bigger picture . . .

Pop: Elbowroom . . . Say, honey, gosh, I don't know what I'd do without you.

Mom: Really?

Pop: Yeah, I mean it, you're special.

Mom: There's no one else in the world like you, either.

Pop: You're my everything.

Mom: Oh, you say the sweetest things.

Pop: But they come from the heart! My plum!

Mom: My hero!

(Just then Junior bounds into the room.)

Junior: Hey, Mom 'n Pop, guess what? I—hey, what is this mush?

Pop: Heh heh. Your Mom and I were just having a friendly chat, as always. But tell me, son, what's on your mind?

Junior: Well, I'm at a loss for words to explain why this is, but while I was upstairs just now, I suddenly found that my musical tastes had matured!

Mom: You mean you've seen the light and no longer love rock 'n' roll?

Junior: Boy, mothers sure are mind readers. You picked my brain! But that's exactly what happened. I decided to put on your old Ray Coniff records at low volume and . . . and I *love* them. I'll never blast my speakers again!

Pop: That's a heartwarming development, son.

(Just then Little Sister skips into the room.)

Sis: Mom! Pop! Guess what?

Mom: I can't! Tell us! We're all ears!

Sis: Well, it was like a bolt from the blue . . . my friends and I came to an understanding that we talk too much in general and that, in specific, we hog the phone disgracefully!

Mom: Mercy on us! From the mouths of babes . . . !

Sis: Not only that, but from now on we're going to confine our conversations to two-minute exchanges of essential information each morning at homeroom.

Mom: Will wonders never cease?

(Just then Junior, who has rushed offstage briefly, leaps back on.)

Junior: I think they're just beginning, Mom.

Pop: Junior! Watch your tongue! Your mother's heart!

Junior: No, really, there are things going on around here that'll really open your eyes!

Mom: That's okay, sweetheart. I live on my children's every word, you know.

Junior: You won't be sorry, Mom, because this news puts the icing on the cake.

Pop: Well, then, for heaven's sake, tell us! The suspense is killing us.

Junior: Okay, here it is. Patches the Cat has stopped sharpening her claws on our sofa! She's decided to sharpen them on the old broken overstuffed chair in the basement and promises never to spoil our good furniture again!

Pop: You don't mean it! Am I hearing things? I've heard everything now.

(Just then, Little Sister, who had skipped offstage, skips back again.)

Sis: Mom! Pop! Hold your hats! This one will knock you flat!

Mom: Tell us, honey. Get it off your chest.

Sis: Well, I know this is hard to swallow, but Snuffles the Golden Retriever somehow figured out what the toilet is for! He just flushed it by twisting the handle in his teeth! He won't be whining or scratching the woodwork anymore!

Mom: I'm speechless!

Pop: I'm tongue-tied!

(Just then, the evening paper flumps on the front porch, the TV set—which has been on throughout the scene—pops into bright focus, and the whole family goes arm-in-arm into the breakfast nook to dine happily on charred hamburgers. Moral: For every cloud there's a silver lining!)

Parents to Kids

THE DARK SIDE

Now, you just hold your horses, young man! Come off it! What's that? . . . Hold your tongue! Don't give me any of your lip! Keep a civil tongue in your head. And if you can't say something nice, don't say anything at all. You never lift a finger to help around here. It's the least you can do, you know. You don't realize you gotta pay your dues, pay the price, do your fair share! So act your age, get your act together, get on the stick, toe the line, and turn over a new leaf before you force me to lay down the law. But why do I have to drum this into your head? Time and time again I've told you. Time after time I've said it. If I've told you once, I've told you a thousand times. I can talk till I'm blue in the face, and what good does it do? You think you can get away with murder. Well, let me tell you a thing or two, I wasn't born yesterday. Why, when I was your age, I helped my mother all the time without even being asked and with a smile on my face too! I'm fed up. I've had it up to here. I won't stand for it. You can get out of my hair is what you can do. You can make yourself scarce. Shape up or ship out. And don't come crying afterward to me. Let it be a lesson to you. You'll have no one to blame but yourself!

Shape up or ship out

THE BRIGHT SIDE

There, there, deary—don't cry over spilt milk. Crying doesn't help. Soldiers don't cry, you know. Try to pull yourself together, get back on your feet, take it in stride, take one thing at a time, and get back on the beam. Now, let me give you a piece of advice, a gentle reminder. You've got a good head on your shoulders, so use it! You can hold your head high. And don't sell yourself short. People won't value you higher than you value yourself. Make the most of it. You owe it to yourself to do your very best. Anything worth doing is worth doing well. Put your best foot forward. Remember, honey, we're with you every step of the way. And you can start by putting on clean underwear. What if you died in a car accident today and people saw you were wearing dirty underwear? Just imagine how you'd feel! Better safe than sorry!

Be sure you put on clean underwear . . .

Bossing

Uh-oh! You've been called out on the carpet. And the boss is about to give you a lot of grief, as for instance, a piece of his mind, a hard time, the business, the bum's rush, a grilling, and the third degree. The boss is lowering the boom. He definitely has the upper hand, he holds all the cards, he's got you over a barrel and is raking you over the coals. He'll put the screws on you. He'll put you in your place. He'll make you knuckle under and cry uncle. He'll walk all over you and ride roughshod over you. He'll ram it down your throat and rub your nose in it. He'll throw his weight around and show you who's boss. I just hope he doesn't show you the door and give you the sack. What if he throws you to the wolves?

The big cheese

Bolstering

Getting fired isn't the end of the world. It could be worse. After all, it happens to the best of us. It comes with the territory. Everyone has his cross to bear—maybe this is yours. Maybe it's a blessing in disguise. So don't lose heart or let it get you down or give it another thought or lose any sleep over it. You'll bounce back, you'll ride out the storm. It'll all blow over. Your ship will come in. And as for jobs, well, you know what they say, there're a lot of fish in the sea. Just put it in perspective and look at the bright side. You know yourself that you've got to lead your own life. Only you can know in your heart of hearts what to do. Your future's in your hands. So keep your chin up, stay in there, keep slugging. You've come a long way. You've

Hitch your wagon to a star

got so much going for you. You're worth your weight in gold. And you look like a million bucks, too, bright-eyed and bushy-tailed, the picture of health. So take a stab at it. It won't hurt to try. No gain without pain—nothing ventured, nothing gained. Where there's a will there's a way. You're only as old as you feel. Your sun hasn't set. So give it 100 percent, your best shot, all you've got. Set your sights high! The sky's the limit! Shoot for the stars! Hitch your wagon to a star.

SECTION THREE

SOURCES

FOOD FOR THOUGHT #5: "A PICTURE IS WORTH A THOUSAND WORDS"

If asked what the source of a certain cliché is, most people automatically start thinking about the historical origin. They assume that by finding out when and where the cliché was first used, they'll understand its source. There are some problems, though, with this approach.

The first is that the historical origin of many clichés is unknown. Compilers of cliché dictionaries, which are designed to trace the history of each entry, readily admit this problem. Their source studies are often mere speculation, guesswork—educated and intriguing, but still guesswork. The cliché "in apple-pie order," for instance, is traced by scholars to various possible sources: the neatness of apple slices arranged in early New England pies; the French phrase *cap à pied,* meaning "from head to foot," and used of a knight in armor; the French phrase *nappes pliées,* meaning "folded linen." All these possibilities, though, are frankly offered in the sourcebooks only as suggestions. The recurrent comment, which runs almost like a refrain through these books, is "origin uncertain."

Even when the historical origin of a cliché is known for certain, however, that information doesn't help us understand why the cliché exists, what made it become a cliché. This is the second problem with the historical approach to cliché sources. "The writing on the wall," for example, clearly comes from the book of Daniel in the Bible; but it's not a cliché *because* it comes from Daniel. If there weren't something in the phrase itself to make it stick, it wouldn't have become a cliché.

What has made this phrase stick is most likely the image it contains. When we "see the writing on the wall," we see large, ominous words looming in front of us on a wide, immovable surface. This powerful picture, rather than any memory of Belshazzar, is what brings the cliché to mind—and to our mouths—when we feel a sense of impending doom. The staying power of many other clichés, too, can be explained by their metaphorical content. They give a picture that grabs us at some level of our consciousness. "In apple-pie order" is a cliché probably because of the sense of hominess and hence of rightness carried by the image of an apple pie. Whether or not the first such pie was made in early New England is irrelevant.

Historical origin is usually irrelevant for understanding the source of clichés, because no phrase is a cliché at its origin. It becomes one only through repeated popular use; it remains one only in the act of collective repetition. The significant source of clichés is, therefore, the popular imagination in which they keep coming to mind. Understanding their source means understanding what brings them to mind.

A catchy metaphor isn't the only quality that keeps a cliché alive in our minds. As other sections of the book suggest, psychological aptness, philosophical validity, or the mere rhythm of the phrase can also account for a cliché's continued appeal. But since the main attraction of many seems to be their metaphor, this entire section of the book is organized around the pictures clichés give.

Not surprisingly, most of these pictures are drawn from the common objects around us. They're grouped on the following pages into three large categories: the natural world (in "It's Only Natural"); our own bodies (in "From Head to Toe"); the products of civilization (in "Civilization: The Staples of Existence"). Individual categories receive further discussion where appropriate, so all that needs to be reemphasized here is the commonness, the familiarity, of the images. Clichés hit home because their images are close to home. Air, water, dogs, flowers, colors, hands, the head, the heart, clothes, money, furniture, food—this is the stuff of life from which clichés come and with which they keep us connected.

Clichés are often accused of being "dead metaphors." They are indeed dead in the sense that the cliché itself is stiff and unchanging. But in another sense they're very much alive: Their metaphors—as it is the purpose of this section to show— are full of life. The life of an entire culture could probably be sketched simply by putting together the pictures contained in its clichés.

It's Only Natural

YOU'RE IN YOUR ELEMENT

In ancient philosophy, all material things were seen as composed of four basic elements: air, earth, fire, and water. The cliché "you're in your element" is probably a holdover from this cosmology; to be in one's element is to be in one's natural place. Though we no longer believe that everything comes from these four elements, we do draw many of our clichés from them. So our minds are still in close touch with these fundamentals of our natural surroundings.

Air

it's up in the air

Let's air this out

a breath of fresh air
a lot of hot air
walking on air
building castles in the air
something's in the air
clear the air
it came out of thin air

                                    reach for the stars
                                    thank your lucky stars
                                    his star is on the wane
                                    he has stars in his eyes
                                        saw stars

his sun has set
make hay while the sun shines
there's nothing new under the sun
his place in the sun
      moment in the sun

                                    praise him to the skies
                                    blow it sky-high
                                    pie in the sky
                                    the sky's the limit

once in a blue moon
ask for the moon
promise the moon

                                    on cloud nine
                                    under a cloud
                                    his head's in the clouds
                                    every cloud has a silver lining

                                    I'm in seventh heaven
                                    I'd move heaven and earth

Earth

down to earth
the salt of the earth
the scum of the earth

keep your ear to the ground
let's get this thing off the ground
has her feet on the ground
covers a lot of ground
cut the ground out from under him
gaining ground/ losing ground
beat it into the ground

as old as the hills
king of the hill
head for the hills
it's an uphill battle
it's all downhill from here
he's over the hill

make mountains out of molehills

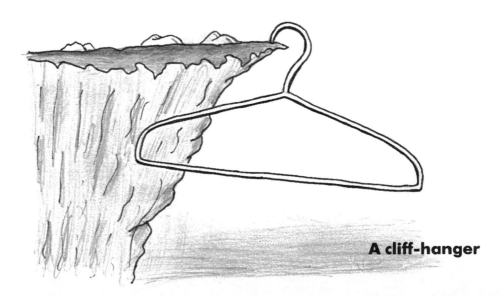

A cliff-hanger

leave them in the dust
bite the dust
the dust is beginning to settle
dry as dust

I feel like dirt

his name is mud
it's clear as mud
a stick-in-the-mud
drag his name through the mud

hides his head in the sand

Fire

she's a ball of fire
        playing with fire
        all fired up about it
the fat's in the fire
too many irons in the fire

Out of the frying pan into the fire

spread like wildfire
he works like a house on fire
he'll never set the world on fire

where there's smoke there's fire
go up in smoke

fan the flames

burn the candle at both ends
can't hold a candle to him

burn the midnight oil
a burning desire
got her fingers burned
money burns a hole in her pocket
that burns me up

Water

keep your head above water
come hell or high water
don't muddy the water
pour oil on troubled waters
throw cold water on it
in a lot of hot water
in deep water
testing the waters
dead in the water
doesn't hold water
watered down
that's water over the dam

he's a long drink of water
blood is thicker than water
take to it like a duck to water
rolls off her like water off a duck's back

get your feet wet
a wet blanket
all washed up
in over my head
swamped with work
it leaves me drained

a drop in the bucket

on thin ice
break the ice
the tip of the iceberg

up a creek without a paddle
sold down the river
a big fish in a small pond
go jump in the lake

I'm at sea
    in dire straits
there are other fish in the sea
as deep as the ocean

made a big splash
take the plunge
went off the deep end

Making waves

the tide turned
swim against the tide

I'm at a low ebb

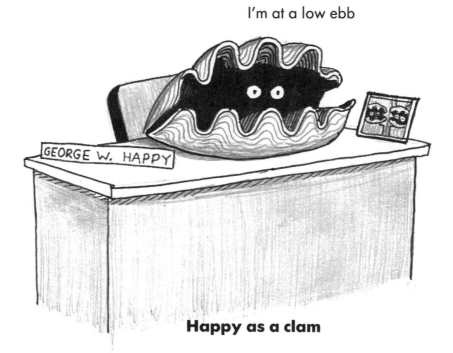

Happy as a clam

FOOD FOR THOUGHT #6: "LIKE A CHICKEN WITH ITS HEAD CUT OFF"

We have an abundance of animal clichés. But almost none of them are actually about animals. Usually they picture some apparently characteristic animal activity, but their real subject is human behavior.

"She's leading a dog's life," "you're living in a pigsty," "he's feathering his nest"—while the image in such clichés is of an animal, the subject is always a person. The animals are being used to describe what we're really interested in: ourselves. This exploitative quality is clearest in the many animal clichés that are similes: She's "quiet as a mouse," "crazy as a loon," "happy as a clam at high tide"; he acts "like a scared rabbit" or "like a chicken with its head cut off"; he "eats like a bird" or "like a horse." Some of the behavior attributed to animals here is obviously just a projection of human attitudes. Are loons really crazy? Or clams happy?

Human activity occasionally becomes the explicit as well as the implicit subject of animal clichés. Examples are "you're beating a dead horse," "he's on his high horse," "she has him on a leash." In such clichés the animal is made to serve human interests twice over: once in the pictured action (the animal being seen as beaten or ridden or led on a leash by a human) and again in the figurative meaning (the whole cliché characterizing someone's behavior as futile or snobbish or controlling).

Animal clichés do more, though, than simply exploit the animal world for our own interest. They also convey a sense of kinship we feel with animal creation. We see animals as close enough to ourselves that we can easily project our behavior on to them and theirs back on to ourselves. Yet they're different enough from us to be able to give us a comic perspective on our behavior.

Animal . . .

Wild Animals

get the lion's share
can't change his stripes
an eager beaver
in a coon's age
monkey see, monkey do

like a herd of elephants
has a memory like an elephant

hungry as a bear

runs like a deer

cry wolf
a lone wolf
throw him to the wolves
keep the wolf from the door

acts like a scared rabbit

Multiply like rabbits

quiet as a mouse
poor as a churchmouse

has bats in her belfry
blind as a bat
like a bat out of hell

smell a rat
it's a rat race

Horses and Cattle

He eats like a horse

wild horses couldn't drag me
hold your horses
a horse of a different color
on his high horse
beating a dead horse
straight from the horse's mouth

don't look a gift horse in the mouth
don't put the cart before the horse
don't change horses in mid-stream

stubborn as a mule

takes the bit between his teeth
keep a tight rein on him

till the cows come home

beef up

strong as an ox
dumb as an ox

got a bum steer

take the bull by the horns
like a bull in a china shop
cock-and-bull story

Insects

put a bug in his ear
snug as a bug in a rug

has ants in his pants

as busy as a bee
make a beeline to

mad as a hornet
stir up a hornet's nest

a fly in the ointment
I'd like to be a fly on the wall
dropping like flies
wouldn't hurt a fly

have butterflies in my stomach

weaving a web of intrigue

Has a bee in her bonnet

Fishes, Snakes, and Worms

that's a fish story
there are other fish in the sea
a big fish in a small pond

Like a fish out of water

he's a cold fish

green around the gills
up to the gills with it

clam up
happy as a clam at high tide

the world is my oyster

he's a real snake in the grass
sharper than a serpent's tooth
deaf as an adder

it's a can of worms

going at a snail's pace

Pigs, Sheep, and Goats

that gets my goat

separate the sheep from the goats

he's the black sheep
may as well be hanged for a sheep as for a lamb

gentle as a lamb
in two shakes of a lamb's tail
return to the fold

live in a pigsty

Go whole hog

put on the hog
living high off the hog
go hog-wild
that's hogwash

you can't make a silk purse out of a sow's ear
don't cast your pearls before swine

Chickens

chicken-hearted

No spring chicken

the chickens have come home to roost
don't count your chickens before they're hatched
like a chicken with its head cut off
naked as a plucked chicken

mad as a wet hen

tough turkey

cock-and-bull story
cock of the walk
proud as a peacock
strutting his stuff

rules the roost
flew the coop
smooth their ruffled feathers

Birds

it's for the birds

Eats like a bird

a little bird told me
a bird in the hand . . .
birds of a feather . . .

as the crow flies
happy as a lark
crazy as a loon
wise as an owl
I don't give a hoot

wild-goose chase
cook his goose

it's duck soup
a sitting duck

a dead duck
took to it like a duck to water
rolled off her like water off a duck's back

clip his wings
sticks in your craw
feathers his nest

Dogs and Cats

Raining cats and dogs

cat's got your tongue
let the cat out of the bag
thinks she's the cat's meow

play cat-and-mouse with
more than one way to skin a cat

looks like the cat that swallowed the canary
    like something the cat dragged in
    weak as a kitten

lead a dog's life
let sleeping dogs lie
going to the dogs
dog-eat-dog
a lucky dog

you can't teach an old dog new tricks

his bark is worse than his bite
barking up the wrong tree

has him on a leash

in the doghouse

. . . Vegetable, Mineral

It might be surprising at first to see so few vegetable and
mineral clichés after the long parade of animal ones. This makes
sense, though, when we realize that clichés tend to describe
behavior: Vegetables and (especially) minerals don't behave
much.

The vegetable category is interpreted broadly here (as it is in "Twenty Questions"), to include all growing things. The relatively large role of the rose is worth noting. Probably its popularity in clichés comes from its strikingly opposite qualities: the strong sweetness and beauty of the flower, the sharp sting of the thorn.

Vegetables

everything's coming up roses
came off smelling like a rose
it's no bed of roses
a rose by any other name
the bloom is off the rose
led down a primrose path

a thorn in her side
it's a thorny issue

nip it in the bud

can't see the forest for the trees
a babe in the woods
not out of the woods yet

This neck of the woods

the apple doesn't fall far from the tree
drives me up a tree
out on a limb
shaking like a leaf

slept like a log
like a bump on a log
as easy as falling off a log

cool as a cucumber   a tough nut to crack
red as a beet   an old chestnut
that's small potatoes
alike as two peas in a pod
doesn't know beans
doesn't amount to a hill of beans

you can't get blood out of a turnip

she's a clinging vine
heard it through the grapevine

gilding the lily
rolling in clover
fresh as a daisy

beat around the bush

a burr under the saddle
go to seed
a straw in the wind

Minerals

has a heart of gold
worth her weight in gold
good as gold
fool's gold
he's a goldmine of information
a golden opportunity

hit rock bottom
slept like a rock
caught between a rock and a hard place

a stone's throw
written in stone
leave no stone unturned
has a heart of stone

the salt of the earth
take it with a grain of salt

diamond in the rough
crystal clear

Fundamental Facts of Life

The reference here isn't to the birds and the bees (already covered in "Animals"), but to other categories of the natural world that play a big part in our consciousness: colors, numbers, temperature, weather, time, life, death.

Showing Your True Colors

that makes me see red
red as a beet
running in the red
paint the town red
doesn't have a red cent
gave him the red-carpet treatment

tickled pink
in the pink

paints a rosy picture
looks through rose-colored glasses

                        green around the gills
                        get the green light
                        have a green thumb
                        turn green with envy

              he's true blue
                  in a blue funk
              once in a blue moon
              talks a blue streak
              talk till I'm blue in the face

black as night
      as pitch
      as the ace of spades
you're in my black book
running in the black
the pot calling the kettle black

we're in a gray area
it's not just black and white

White as a ghost

White as a sheet

We've Got Your Number

—You can count on it!

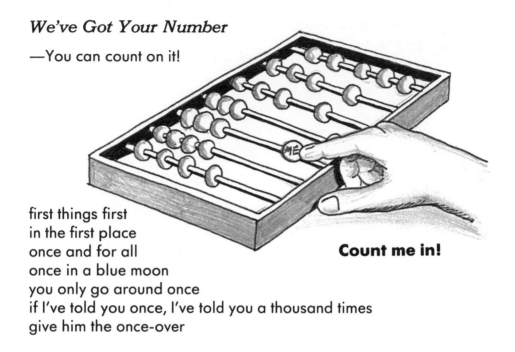

Count me in!

first things first
in the first place
once and for all
once in a blue moon
you only go around once
if I've told you once, I've told you a thousand times
give him the once-over

on second thought
plays second fiddle
it's second nature to me

think twice about it

gave him the third degree

in seventh heaven

at the eleventh hour

to the *n*th degree

you're one in a million
        one of a kind
        one for the books
it takes one to know one
it's just one of those things

one thing at a time
a one-shot deal
one hand washes the other

One foot in the grave

He's got all his eggs in one basket
if you've seen one, you've seen them all
we're back at square one
look out for number one

two can play at that game
it takes two to tango
he has two strikes against him
he's two-faced

He's got two left feet

two heads are better than one
I'm of two minds about it
I'll show them a thing or two
there's no two ways about it
it's a two-way street
it's the lesser of two evils
put two and two together
in two shakes of a lamb's tail
alike as two peas in a pod

two's company, three's a crowd

staring at the four walls

it's six of one, half a dozen of the other
six feet under

at sixes and sevens

behind the eight ball

on cloud nine
a stitch in time saves nine

twenty-twenty hindsight

gave it one hundred percent

never in a thousand years
if I've told you once, I've told you a thousand times

thanks a million
I'd give a million dollars
you look like a million bucks
you're a million laughs
you're one in a million

He Blows Hot and Cold

he's full of hot air
    in a lot of hot water
    hot under the collar

she thinks she's hot stuff
can't take the heat

they're going at it hot and heavy
it's a hot potato

Strike while the iron is hot

give them a warm welcome
it warms the cockles of my heart

cool, calm, and collected
cool as a cucumber
cooling his heels
he's Joe Cool
    a cold fish
    left out in the cold
throw cold water on it
cold hands, warm heart
get cold feet
    the cold shoulder
it makes my blood run cold

Under the Weather

as right as rain
it's raining cats and dogs
it never rains but it pours
got the rainy-day blues
save it for a rainy day

            I haven't the foggiest idea

I'm snowed under
he doesn't have a snowball's chance in hell

            it's the calm before the storm
            we'll weather the storm
               ride out the storm

he's a fair-weather friend

he stole your thunder
it's a bolt out of the blue

it's in the wind
a straw in the wind
throw caution to the wind

shoot the breeze
it's a breeze

It will blow over

FOOD FOR THOUGHT #7: "HAVING THE TIME OF MY LIFE"

Among the most fundamental facts of life that clichés draw on are "time," "death," and "life" itself. These concepts are so basic, and at the same time so abstract, that they seem to call for some reflection. Here, then, instead of just lists, is a running commentary on what these words are up to in clichés.

It's Just a Matter of Time

"Time" in clichés has a few different functions. It can be a process perceived as outside us, a process we're advised to accept patiently, to let be:

> all in good time
> only time will tell
> for the time being
> stood the test of time
> it's just a matter of time

"Time" in the plural, though also perceived as outside us, is less a process than an environment. Such "times" are a given, whose qualities we must simply accept:

> there are tough times ahead
> it's a sign of the times
> behind the times
> going through rough times

In contrast to the "time" or "times" that are a given, there's a "time" that clichés urge us to take hold of, to seize, to act on. This "time" is opportunity:

It's high time

it's a race against time
time is running out
time's a-wasting
time flies
a stitch in time saves nine
just in the nick of time

Living on borrowed time

If we miss the opportunity, there's a sense of loss or of being at loose ends:

>I've got time on my hands
>I'm just killing time
>better luck next time

"I've got time on my hands" expresses a different attitude from "all in good time"—boredom as opposed to patience—but both are attitudes toward time itself. Some clichés, though, simply use "time" to express an attitude toward something else. It might be exasperation at others' behavior:

>time and time again I've told you
>don't give me a hard time
>one thing at a time
>I wouldn't give her the time of day

or pleasure for oneself:

>I'm having the time of my life!

Clichés with words pointing to units or periods of time—"moment," "day," "year"—fall into similar categories, though with slightly different nuances. As a process outside us, these periods sound a bit burdensome:

>day in and day out
>year in, year out
>working night and day

In the plural, like "times," these periods take on qualities of their own:

> we've seen better days
> I gave her the best years of my life

As opportunity, the unit of time has *already* been seized:

> her moment in the sun
> the moment of truth
> on the spur of the moment
> never a dull moment
> you've saved the day
> you've made my day
> this is my lucky day

or made the most of:

> we've put in a good day's work
> let's call it a day
> another day, another dollar

or lost:

> this isn't my day

And as with "time," the period can be used to express a strong emotion:

> never in a thousand years!

It's a Matter of Life or Death

"Life" in clichés can also be a period of time:

> she's in the prime of life
> he lived a long, full life

But since it's a special, finite period of time with personal value (you only go around once), it's treated with a sense of urgency:

> you take your life in your hands

She risked life and limb

> she came within an inch of her life
> it's a matter of life or death

Because it does matter so much, "life" is the subject of philosophical concern. Clichés advise us to

> live life to the fullest
> live and let live
> live and learn

And they pass judgment on *how* we live. It's good to

> lead your own life

and bad to

> lead a dog's life

It's nice to be

    the life of the party

lucky to

    live the life of Riley

important to

    look alive

"Life" is so full of value that it can almost mean reality itself, as when something is

    true to life
    larger than life

What makes us aware of the value of life is death. Death is what cuts life off, so it's not surprising that "death" in clichés commonly expresses a sense of loss, whether loss of physical energy:

Dead tired

dead on his feet
dead to the world
half dead

or loss of health:

looks like death warmed over
like he's at death's door

or loss of opportunity or possibility:

Dead in the water

a dead duck
signed his own death warrant

Nor is it surprising that the other main meaning of "death" in clichés is finality, completion, absoluteness. When

I'm dead sure
he's dead set against it
you're dead wrong
she stopped dead in her tracks

we're using *dead* to mean "absolutely." The absolute end is called

the kiss of death

An odd variety of activities reach their extreme, their limit, in "death." I can be

> bored to death
> scared to death
> tickled to death

What's surprising in these clichés isn't what they say about death but their attitude toward it. Death isn't taken seriously in them. Of course clichés are never deadly serious; it's not in their nature. But even the sentimentality of some "life" clichés ("live life to its fullest") is missing from the ones that use "death." To say "he's a dead weight" or "a dead-head" is not a serious censure. We never say, "This'll be the death of me" if it really will.

It's true that "life" can be treated with equal frivolity. When I say "I'd stake my life on it," I certainly wouldn't. And it's a toss-up whether I express my resolve "over my dead body" or "not on your life!" But whereas "life" is treated philosophically in many clichés, "death" is always treated as a joke. "I could've died laughing" says it all, hits the nail on the head. In fact, I'm most likely to say I could've died laughing when I'm having the time of my life.

From Head to Toe

The human body is the metaphorical source of an amazing number of clichés: easily over three hundred. No doubt the plethora of body parts in our clichés is due to the fact that our body is—well—so close at hand. Looking for an image to express an idea or an experience, we find it right here at our fingertips, right in front of our eyes, as plain as the nose on our face.

   What follows, then, is an anatomy lesson—with body clichés presented, naturally, in order from head to toe.

HEAD

Off the top of my head
I'd say: let's put our heads together
        two heads are better than one
        if your head is screwed on the right way
        you can hold your head up high
        you'll keep your head above water
        and won't get in over your head

But if you let it go to your head
        or let it turn your head
        you'll have a swelled head
        and it'll be hanging over your head

It's okay to laugh your head off
But if you lose your head
     or go head over heels
     or hide your head in the sand
     or have your head in the clouds

          Then you oughta have your head examined
           and I'll have to drum it into your head
           but I need that like a hole in the head

          It's like beating my head against the wall

          Can't you get that through your head?

You're making my hair turn gray
I'm tearing my hair out
Get out of my hair!

But I'll let my hair down
I don't want to split hairs
or make your hair stand on end

We're just a hair's breadth away

          I'm racking my brains
           beating my brains

          I could beat your brains out

Picking your brain

What's on your mind?

                    Speak your mind
                    Have an open mind
                    Have a mind of your own

I can read your mind
You need peace of mind
You've got a lot on your mind
You're of two minds about it
You don't know your own mind
Make up your mind
Mind over matter

                    or it'll drive you out of your mind
                      you'll lose your mind

It's fresh in my mind
It just crossed my mind

I've got half a mind
                    to give you a piece of my mind

It boggles my mind
We need a meeting of minds

Out of sight, out of mind

That's a load off my mind

FACE

Let's face it,

The face in clichés can mean honesty:
            if you face up to it
                    face the music
                    meet face-to-face

Though it might show more than you wish:

            if you put on a long face
            or have guilt written all over your face
            you wouldn't dare to show your face
            you could talk till you're blue in the face

The face can also act as your cover:

you can put the best face on it
       save face
       be poker-faced
         two-faced
       even tell a bold-faced lie

Keep a straight face

If you're caught in the act, though, the face

      does an about-face

           you lose face
              get egg on your face

          it's a slap in the face

EARS

Are you all ears?

I don't want it to fall on deaf ears
          or to go in one ear and out the other

      So, if you turn a deaf ear

I'll bend your ear
    put a bug in your ear
    give you an earful
    even pin back your ears
    and chew your ear

till it's coming down around your ears
    or coming out of your ears

Are your ears burning?

You aren't dry behind the ears

Are you up to your ears in it?
Keep your ear to the ground
Play it by ear

If the walls had ears . . .

Can you believe your ears?

EYES

Here's a real eye-opener:

Don't bat an eye

Keep your eyes peeled
Keep a sharp eye out for
Do it with your eyes open
      in the wink of an eye

There's more here than meets the eye:

You needn't have eyes in the back of your head
      to catch someone's eye

And we needn't go at it eyeball-to-eyeball
      even if we don't see eye-to-eye

And you can cry your eyes out
      and still be a sight for sore eyes

Feast your eyes on this:

Your eyes are bigger than your stomach

You have stars in your eyes

I'm pulling the wool over your eyes

NOSE

It's right under your nose:

You can follow your nose
    or be led around by the nose

Plain as the nose on your face

You can hit it right on the nose
    or cut off your nose to spite your face

You can have a nose for it
    or get your nose rubbed in it

and keep your nose to the grindstone
  or pay through the nose
    and not see beyond your nose
      let it go on right under your nose

Keep your nose clean

You can stick your nose in my business
        thumb your nose at me
        turn up your nose at me
        look down your nose at me

                              It's no skin off *my* nose!

MOUTH

It goes without saying
      that every word out of my mouth is a cliché

And though a few "mouth" clichés refer to eating—

it makes my mouth water
it leaves a bitter taste in my mouth
I'm living from hand to mouth
butter wouldn't melt in his mouth—

Most are indeed about words:
for you can

put words into my mouth
shoot your mouth off
foam at the mouth
talk out of both sides of your mouth
be down in the mouth
put your foot in your mouth
put your money where your mouth is

And except for keeping a stiff upper lip
the lip also stands for speaking:
for you can

pay lip service
or button your lip

Don't give me any of your lip

The tongue, too, is always about talking:
          whether you're tongue-tied
          or the cat's got your tongue
          or it's on the tip of your tongue
          or you speak tongue-in-cheek
          or you cause tongues to wag
          or you hold your tongue
          or you bite your tongue

I do hope you keep a civil tongue in your head

It'll set your teeth on edge
          to sink your teeth into
               "teeth" clichés
  since they're armed to the teeth
          with a fighting, biting spirit:
          fighting tooth-and-nail
          sharper than a serpent's tooth
          the law has teeth in it
          takes the bit between his teeth
          cut your teeth on it
          get your teeth into it

though not all "teeth" clichés have such bite in them:
          it's like pulling teeth
          I'd give my eyeteeth

and you can get out of this
          by the skin of your teeth

NECK AND THROAT

In this neck of the woods, there's a lot of violence:

You can break your neck getting there
You're a pain in the neck

You've got to stick your neck out

You can cut your own throat
I'll ram it down your throat

It's so sad, it gives me a lump in my throat

Whether we're at each other's throats
    or we're running neck-and-neck
        I've got you breathing down my neck

I'm up to my neck in it . . .

SHOULDERS AND ARMS

I can place the blame on your shoulders

Because shoulders are high, they're like pride—

so you stand head and shoulders above the rest

He's got a good head on his shoulders

Because shoulders are expressive—
   you can give someone the cold shoulder
      or rub shoulders with him
      or have a chip on your shoulder

Because arms are long—
  I can keep you at arm's length
    or twist your arm

Because arms hug—
  I can welcome you with open arms

Because of medical practice—
  I can give you a shot in the arm

It cost an arm and a leg

I'd give my right arm
  to have more elbowroom for this

HANDS

With respect to the hand itself,
you can

> give me a hand
> give me the back of your hand
> know something like the back of your hand
> have me eating out of your hand

Bite the hand that feeds you

> have the world in the palm of your hand
> have the upper hand

Caught with his hand in the cookie jar

be an old hand at something
try your hand at it
have a hand in it
dismiss it out of hand
let it get out of hand

Or, since you have two hands, you might find that

one hand washes the other
the right hand doesn't know what the left is doing
things go hand in hand

Or, joining your hands, you might

find that your hands are tied
have your hands full

have time on your hands
get your hands dirty
wash your hands of the whole situation
throw up your hands
take matters into your own hands
take the law into your own hands
take your life into your hands

I've got to hand it to you
This is a real handful
And you're not getting it handed to you on a silver platter
You have to work your fingers to the bone to get it

Speaking of which, we now subdivide the hand into fingers,
so you can

keep your fingers crossed
get your fingers burned

Or, subdividing further, you can

have a finger in every pie
point your finger at me
have me wrapped around your finger
not lift a finger to help
keep your finger on the pulse of the situation
put your finger on it
have it at your fingertips

Or, subdividing still further, you can

be all thumbs
twiddle your thumbs

thumb your nose at me
have me under your thumb
have a green thumb
stick out like a sore thumb

A quick thumbnail sketch

HEART

To get right to the heart of the matter:

You should

> have a heart of gold
> find it in your heart
> be young at heart
> throw yourself into it heart-and-soul
> take heart
> (but don't take it to heart
> or lose heart)

If you wear your heart on your sleeve
   you might lose your heart to someone
      who doesn't have a heart
     or has a heart of stone

But if your heart isn't in it
   you can have a change of heart
      set your heart on it
      do it to your heart's content

Since we can have a heart-to-heart talk
      or a hearty handshake

A man after my own heart

And I hope with all my heart
    from the bottom of my heart
    in my heart of hearts
            that you won't ever be sick at heart
               eat your heart out
               cry your heart out

My heart goes out to you
It makes my heart bleed
It breaks my heart
              to think that your heart might be heavy
                                              or sink
              or your heart might leap into your throat

But—cross my heart—
    it does my heart good
    and warms the cockles of my heart
        to see that your heart's in the right place

and you know all this by heart

BACK AND FRONT

I'll shout it at the top of my lungs:

Get it off your chest!
Make a clean breast of it!

Get off my back

Now, you're the backbone of society
and I've bent over backward for you
and offered to scratch your back while you scratch mine
with my back against the wall
which is a real backbreaker

Then, as soon as my back is turned,
you turn your back on me
    stab me in the back
    behind my back

It simply turns my stomach
I've got butterflies in my stomach
I can't stomach it

I expect you to know this backward and forward

It fell into my lap

LEG

Shake a leg!
Do a lot of legwork
Stop pulling my leg
I have a hollow leg
I'm on my last legs

Doesn't have a leg to stand on

I learned it at my mother's knee
It's a knee-jerk reaction

> to shoot from the hip

FEET

Here we are, finally, finding our feet

so let's jump in with both feet
because with both of your feet, you can

keep your feet on the ground
stand on your own two feet
think on your feet
get your feet wet
get swept off your feet
get back on your feet

Or, less confidently, you can

get cold feet
have two left feet
drag your feet
be dead on your feet
fall at my feet

Whereas with just one foot, you can

have one foot in the grave
put your foot in your mouth
put your foot down
put your best foot forward
start off on the right foot
wait on me hand and foot

Get a foot in the door

With your heels alone, you can

    kick up your heels
    take to your heels
    cool your heels
    dig your heels in
    get set back on your heels

And, last but not least, you can

    keep me on my toes
    toe the line

    and go from HEAD TO TOE

Tread on my toes

PHYSICAL ACTIVITIES

You're probably jumping out of your skin by now,
You're sick of staring at the four walls
You're ready to scream bloody murder
After all, you're only flesh and blood
And your nerves are on edge

I feel it in my bones
You need to show some muscle
You've gotta get moving
So here's your chance to do a song and dance

First, sit up and take note:
                        you're sitting pretty
                                on top of the world

Now, stand tall
        stand your ground
        stand up to everyone

                        (if you give me a lame excuse,
                                I won't stand for it)

Stand up and be counted

Walk all over them
You'll be walking on air
Take it in stride
Make great strides

Now, you should jump at the chance
                jump on the bandwagon
                jump ship
                jump the gun
                jump to conclusions
                go jump in the lake

Ah, there's no rest for the weary
We'll lay it to rest
Let's sleep on it

Civilization: The Staples of Existence

FOOD FOR THOUGHT #8: "THERE'S PLENTY MORE WHERE THESE CAME FROM"

We live our daily lives in a world mostly of our own making. Paradoxically, our natural environment is largely artificial. We're surrounded by the products of civilization. These products include not only objects (clothes, cars, cash) but also activities evidently basic to civilized life (jobs, sports, wars). Nearly all the products of civilization are taken up as metaphors for clichés.

CIVILIZED SOURCES

Clothes

keep it under your hat
hold onto your hat
I'll eat my hat
at the drop of a hat
that's old hat

I tip my hat to you

has a bee in her bonnet

it's a feather in your cap

keep your shirt on
you'll lose your shirt
he's a stuffed shirt
she'd give you the shirt off her back

Hot under the collar

has something up her sleeve
wear your heart on your sleeve
roll up your sleeves and get to work

                                fits like a glove
                                handle with kid gloves
                                goes hand-in-glove with

off the cuff

                                cute as a button
                                button your lip

tied to his mother's apron strings
have it under my belt
tighten my belt a notch

                                who wears the pants in the family?
                                has ants in his pants
                                caught with his pants down
                                scare the pants off
                                that's a kick in the pants

money burns a hole in his pocket

                                too big for his breeches

washes her dirty linen in public

                                it'll knock your socks off

hanging by a thread
wearing myself ragged
coming apart at the seams

if the shoe fits, wear it
the shoe fits the other foot
I wouldn't want to be in her shoes
comfortable as an old shoe
fill his shoes
wait for the other shoe to drop

down at the heels

living on a shoestring

pulled himself up by his bootstraps

Housing and Furnishings

everything but the kitchen sink

set your house in order
like a house on fire

Clichés that hit home:

a house is not a home
ate us out of house and home

The chickens have come home to roost

it's nothing to write home about
bring home the bacon
make yourself at home
there's no place like home
too close to home

get in on the ground floor
doesn't have much upstairs
hit the ceiling
raise the roof

every nook and cranny

the door swings both ways
get your foot in the door
at death's door
the door's still open
closed the door on him
showed him the door
placed the blame at my doorstep

A skeleton in the closet

it's like talking to the wall
beating my head against the wall
staring at the four walls
climbing the walls

has his back against the wall
the writing's on the wall
off the wall
if the walls had ears

go down the drain

he made his bed, let him lie in it
got out of bed on the wrong side

he's a wet blanket

off his rocker

get the red-carpet treatment
call him out on the carpet

pull the rug out from under him
snug as a bug in a rug

Sweep it under the rug

Money

to coin a phrase . . .

a penny for your thoughts
pinching pennies
pay a pretty penny
bright as a new penny   the price is right
                                         pay the price
                                             the piper
                                             your dues

don't have a red cent
put your two cents in   I don't buy that

not worth a plug nickel

Don't take any wooden nickels

don't sell yourself short
sold on the idea

nickel-and-diming

a dime a dozen
stop on a dime

it's money in the bank
I wouldn't bank on it
break the bank

as sound as a dollar
another day, another dollar
bet your bottom dollar

get a blank check

I'd give a million bucks to . . .
looks like a million bucks

in mint condition
take it at face value
the other side of the coin
can't make heads or tails of it

get your money's worth
give him a run for his money
put your money where your mouth is

Food, Cooking, Eating

Food

flat as a pancake
bring home the bacon
a bunch of baloney

gone bananas
sour grapes

an apple a day
an apple-polisher
one rotten apple spoils the barrel
how do you like *them* apples?
life's a bowl of cherries
she's a real peach
a peaches-and-cream complexion
that's peachy

that takes the cake
have your cake and eat it too
nutty as a fruitcake
it's a piece of cake
the icing on the cake

that's the way the cookie crumbles

like taking candy from a baby

don't cry over spilt milk
it's not my cup of tea
crying in his beer

want an egg in your beer?

don't put all your eggs in one basket
get egg on your face
he's a good egg
walking on eggs

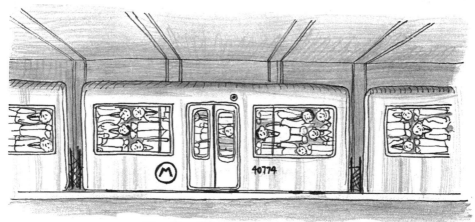

Packed in like sardines

variety is the spice of life
doesn't cut the mustard
in a pickle
slower than molasses

he's a meat-and-potatoes man
a hot potato
in a stew
it's duck soup
don't spill the beans

half a loaf is better than none
knows which side her bread is buttered on
butter him up

pie in the sky
a finger in every pie
in apple-pie order

Cooking

the pot calling the kettle black
out of the frying pan into the fire
stewing in his own juices
put it on the back burner
that'll cook his goose
that's a fine kettle of fish
have other fish to fry

boil it down
mull it over

too many cooks spoil the broth

Eating

eat your heart out
I'll eat my hat
has him eating out of her hand
eat your words
eat crow
eat humble pie
swallow your pride
that's hard to swallow

You are what you eat

bit off more than he could chew
       chew it over
       chew the fat
       chew his ear

                   feast your eyes
              it's either feast or famine
                   I'm fed up

               I'm a glutton for punishment

Sports

he's a team player
he plays by the book
he's always on the sidelines
        out of my league
        in the big leagues

that's the name of the game
at this stage of the game
you win some, you lose some
you can't win 'em all
I'll take a raincheck

it's a toss-up
let's get the ball rolling
that's the way the ball bounces
you'll bounce back
catch you on the rebound
he's on the ball

The ball is in your court

he's out in left field
he plays hardball
   struck out
   won't get to first base
   went to bat for her
   threw her a curve ball
right off the bat
it's a whole new ballgame
a ballpark figure

He has two strikes against him

throw your hat in the ring
don't hit a man when he's down
keep in there slugging
roll with the punches
that's hitting below the belt
you hit it right on the nose
she's a knockout
he's a heavy hitter
I took it on the chin
  feel punchy
  beat him to the punch
  threw in the towel
saved by the bell

you're in the running
     off to a running start
don't jump the gun
toe the line
clear the first hurdle
she has the inside track
   has a good track record
it's down to the wire

               give it your best shot
               have a shot at it
               it's a long shot
               call the shots

par for the course

               I'm behind the eight ball
               she plays all the angles

               you're not pulling your weight

               get back on the beam

War, Weapons, Violence

enough food to feed an army
rise up through the ranks
pull rank
do an about-face
he's a real trooper
he swears like a trooper

it's just a shot in the dark
he goes off half-cocked
   shoots from the hip
   shoots his big mouth off
he's up in arms
    armed to the teeth

come under fire
the news was a bombshell
rally round the flag
going great guns
stand your ground
stick to your guns
come through with flying colors
fight a losing battle
fight to the bitter end
a last-ditch effort
beat a retreat
bury the hatchet
bury our dead

He burned his bridges

let's zero in on it
we're right on target

          lock, stock, and barrel
          it's a surefire solution
              a smoking gun

bite the bullet

straight as an arrow

          kill time
          kill with kindness
          get away with murder
          scream bloody murder
          take a stab at it
          it's a stab in the back
          beat it into his head
          beaten to a pulp
          beat my head against the wall
          don't beat a dead horse

don't break your neck to get there
it breaks my heart
I'll break the back of this thing yet

          here's the kicker
          I could kick myself
          get a kick out of it
          that's a kick in the pants

she knocked herself out for us
this'll knock you off your feet
knock your socks off
knock the stuffing out of him

when push comes to shove
twist his arm
fighting tooth-and-nail
cut off her nose to spite her face
cut your own throat
ram it down their throats
they won't know what hit them

it's a slap in the face
lashed out at us
drag it out of him

rake them over the coals
draw blood

We had a blast

Occupations

it's all in a day's work

hammer out an agreement
hit the nail on the head
nail it down
he's hard as nails
    dead as a doornail
    sharp as a tack

Got a screw loose somewhere

it's a nuts-and-bolts issue
it goes against the grain
he isn't holding up his end
she's on the level
    at the cutting edge
    lost her edge
she threw a monkey wrench into the works
    has an axe to grind
    flew off the handle
it hit me like a ton of bricks

                    he's sowing his wild oats
                    has a long row to hoe

make hay while the sun shines
reap the benefits

put him out to pasture
till the cows come home
closing the barn door after the cows got out

it's grist for the mill
grind it out

strike while the iron is hot
has too many irons in the fire

fish or cut bait
fishing for compliments
took it hook, line, and sinker
that's a fish story
a good catch

mend your ways
on the mend
patch over our differences
iron out our differences
dyed in the wool   have it all sewn up
run of the mill   a stitch in time

play it by ear
play second fiddle to
toots his own horn
pull out all the stops
tune him out
end on a sour note

it's on the drawing board
put on the finishing touches

back to the salt mines

it's business as usual

Don't paint yourself into a corner

CLEARANCE SALE

start with a clean slate

get down to brass tacks

blow the whistle on him

take him down a peg or two
put the screws on
razor-sharp

the key to my heart

knock on wood

Stiff as a board

go out like a light

a head like a sieve
a mind like a steel trap

clear as a bell
doesn't ring a bell

like clockwork
a race against the clock
turn back the clock

as light as a feather

go fly a kite
high as a kite

go through it with a fine-tooth comb

look through rose-colored glasses

put *that* in your pipe and smoke it

a barrel of laughs
scrape the bottom of the barrel
kick the bucket
a drop in the bucket

prick his balloon

bald as a billiard ball

reinvent the wheel

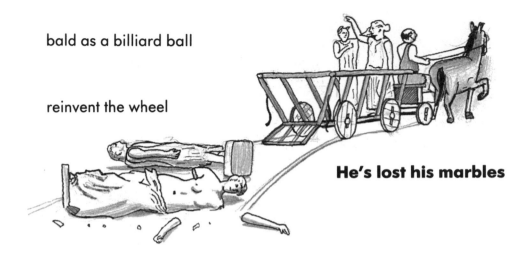

He's lost his marbles

hand it to him on a silver platter

caught with his hand in the cookie jar

the cup is either half full or half empty

GEORGE W. LIMP

Limp as a dishrag

smooth as silk

a needle in a haystack
on pins and needles
don't pin your hopes on it
so quiet you could hear a pin drop

with all the trimmings

it's in the bag

that about wraps it up

URBAN ENVIRONMENT

on automatic pilot
let's get this thing off the ground

like ships passing in the night
missed the boat
all in the same boat
left high and dry

as much as the traffic will bear
doesn't take a backseat to anyone
in the driver's seat
backseat driver
get some mileage out of it

Get the green light

on easy street
right up my alley
pave the way

we'll cross that bridge when we come to it
bridge the gap
he'll try to sell you the Brooklyn Bridge

at the helm
give a wide berth to
on an even keel
steer a steady course
take the wind out of his sails
go full-speed ahead
jump ship
don't go overboard
don't give up the ship

Your ship will come in

set the stage for
fill the bill
behind the scenes
in the limelight
right on cue
face the music
has her act together
a tough act to follow
gave them a song and dance
a showstopper
let's get this show on the road
I'll show them who's running this show

Brought down the house

you can't fight City Hall
don't make a federal case out of it
run it up the flagpole and see who salutes

lock him up and throw away the key

the school of hard knocks

right in your own backyard
it's no picnic
mend fences

in for the long haul
asleep at the switch
the wrong side of the tracks
the light at the end of the tunnel

Obsolete Customs and Past Cultures

This whole section on "Sources" has focused on the metaphorical source of clichés—all the images from everyday life that clichés are drawn from. The section now closes with some clichés that, while coming from daily life, come from that of days gone by. The custom or practice that the cliché refers to is dead and gone, yet the cliché remains alive.

"He bit the dust" is an example. The phrase comes from Homeric warfare, in which the losing fighter was often speared from his chariot head downward or otherwise thrust over by his opponent's weapon, so that at the moment of death he literally "bit the dust." We no longer practice warfare this way, and we wouldn't have the cliché either if—to repeat a main point of this book—the phrase didn't capture our imagination. The image of biting dust is disgusting and degrading; the very sound of the short clipped words and the final *t*'s has a ring of finality. (There's more on the sound of clichés in the next section.) Quick and sharp, together they convey a sense of humiliating defeat. This is the same sense the phrase had in Homer, so the cliché has managed to carry on the phrase's meaning long after the culture it came from is gone. In such cases, reminding ourselves of the historical origin can help us understand the cliché's appeal, especially if—as some theorists suggest—a hint of the original custom hangs on to the phrase in our collective unconscious.

So while this section on "Sources" opened with a disclaimer of the importance of historical sources for understanding the life of clichés, it closes with a partial disclaimer of *that* disclaimer. Following are the origins of some clichés that come from obsolete customs and past cultures. For clichés where the original custom is obvious, no historical note is added. For those with notes, the historical information has been borrowed from several books: Charles Earle Funk, *A Hog on Ice* and *Heavens to Betsy;* Charles Lurie, *Everyday Sayings;* Neil Ewart, *Everyday Phrases;* William and Mary Morris, *Dictionary of Word and Phrase Origins;* James Rogers, *The Dictionary of Clichés* and *Brewer's Dictionary of Phrase and Fable*. All these books are delightful to browse in and are full of fascinating speculation—and even some facts—on the history of selected clichés.

SOCIOECONOMIC LIFE

"he who pays the piper calls the tune"

>   From a practice of medieval entertainment.

"when my ship comes in"

>   From the days when merchant traders waited for their ships to return full of goods they could sell.

"let it go by the board"

>   From sailing-ship days. If a mast broke in a storm, the skipper might decide to let it go by the board (the side of the ship) into the sea.

"pull up stakes"

>   From colonial New England, when a settler who was dissatisfied with the parcel of land allotted to him pulled up the boundary stakes and moved elsewhere.

"go to town"

> From the pioneer and rural days of American culture, when going to town meant a shopping and socializing spree.

"upset the apple cart"

> From days when roads to the market were bumpy, and the loss of a load of valuable apples was serious.

"don't put all your eggs in one basket"

> In case you drop the basket.

"get down to brass tacks"

> From the practice in drapers' shops when, after the customer had chosen a cloth, the shop assistant would measure it against brass-headed nails evenly spaced along the counter.

"get the sack"

> From the practice of handing back to workmen their toolsacks when firing them from their job.

"it's highway robbery"

EVERYDAY SOCIAL LIFE

"dead as a doornail"

> From the days before electric doorbells, when visitors pounded with a door knocker on a metal plate attached to the door by a nail. From being constantly pounded on the head, the nail was said to have all the life knocked out of it.

"pull the wool over his eyes"

> From the days of powdered wigs, which were jokingly pulled down over the wearer's eyes to keep him from seeing something.

PRACTICES OF WAR, TORTURE, PUNISHMENT, AND OPPRESSION

"the crack in his armor"

"hoist on one's own petard"

> From the danger of firing this ancient instrument of war, the petard, which when hoisted to blow up high obstacles often blew up the firer as well.

"hold the fort"

"bury the hatchet"

> From the American Indian practice of burying their hatchets and scalping knives, while smoking the peace pipe, in order to bury past hostilities.

"put the screws on"

> From the seventeenth-century European torture of clamping a victim's thumb under screws, which were slowly tightened to extort confession under pressure of the pain.

"haul over the coals"

> From British kings' practice of slowly dragging victims over burning coals.

"run the gauntlet"

> From the practice among soldiers and sailors of punishing a cowardly colleague by making him run between rows of men as they all tried to whip him.

"may as well be hanged for a sheep as for a lamb"

> From the days when both thefts were punished by hanging, so thieves went after the more valuable animal, the sheep.

"in one's black book"

From the practice among British authorities of listing names of offenders in a black book. The first such book was Henry VIII's list of monasteries, which he charged with "sin, vicious, carnal, and abominable living" as a pretext for dissolving them and taking over their land.

"sold down the river"

From the American slavery practice of selling slaves down the Mississippi River to plantations in the Deep South, where slaves were treated more harshly.

THE IMPORTANCE OF THE HORSE TO DAILY LIFE

"don't change horses in the middle of the stream"

"ride roughshod over"

From the practice of riding horses with the nailheads of the horseshoes left projecting, so that the horse could go anywhere without slipping.

"put the cart before the horse"

From as far back as ancient Rome, where the expression for getting things reversed was "the plow draws the oxen."

"put your shoulder to the wheel"

From the effort of the carter to help his horse pull the wagon out of a rut by pushing the cartwheel himself.

"my old stamping ground"

From the custom of leaving one's horse to stamp around while waiting in a place one frequently visited.

ENERGY SOURCES

"running out of steam"

"burning the midnight oil"

"burning the candle at both ends"

PAGEANTRY

"rest on one's laurels"

> From the ancient Greek practice of giving a wreath of laurels to the victor in the Pythian Games.

"on his high horse"

> From the practice, as far back as the fourteenth century, of people of the highest rank parading on the tallest horses.

"take him down a peg"

> From the eighteenth-century British navy custom of using a system of pegs to raise or lower a ship's flags according to the degree of honor being conferred on someone.

"jump on the bandwagon"

> From the American political-campaign practice, made obsolete by television campaigning, of candidates' parading in a bandwagon onto which people would jump to show their support.

SOUNDS

FOOD FOR THOUGHT #10: "IN ONE EAR AND OUT THE OTHER"

Clichés do indeed go in one ear and out the other. But they wouldn't remain clichés if something didn't keep drawing them back to our ear again, pulling them through our minds and out our mouths over and over. For many clichés, their power to attract us lies at least partly in the way they sound: their rhythm, their rhyme, their repetition of consonants or of whole words. So while section three grouped clichés according to the pictures with which they appeal to our mind's eye, section four gathers them according to their appeal to our ear.

Of course some clichés appeal to both eye and ear. "Bald as a billiard ball"; "hold your horses"; "burned his bridges": these are catchy because of their images as well as their alliteration. Similarly, repetition of a word can reinforce through the ear a picture that strikes the eye: "home sweet home," "monkey see, monkey do," "go at it eyeball-to-eyeball," "have a heart-to-heart talk."

Monkey see, monkey do

Yet many clichés seem to strike us through their sound alone. Without the alliteration of the following phrases, for instance, it's hard to imagine that they'd have become clichés: "tit for tat," "cutting it close," "safe and sound," "on the tip of my tongue," "wouldn't touch it with a ten-foot pole." In this last one, it's likely that either "touch" is what gives us the "ten," or "ten" is what gives us the "touch": If the phrase had developed with a nine-foot pole, no doubt we "wouldn't get near it" or "wouldn't nudge it."

Another rhetorical quality that has raised many phrases to cliché-hood is rhyme, which is certainly the claim to fame of "fair and square," "pie in the sky," "by hook or by crook," "that takes the cake," "that's the name of the game." Inner rhyme (assonance), too, though less catchy, still grabs the ear enough to make clichés of "save the day," "jump the gun," "down and out," "nice try." In all cases of alliterative or rhymed clichés, what catches our ear is the repeated sound. The repetition of initial consonant, inner vowel, or final vowel and consonant pulls the words together so that they stick both in the phrase and in our minds.

For clichés with whole words repeated, this is certainly the main force of their attraction. "First things first," "hope against hope," "boys will be boys," "call a spade a spade," "on the up and up": the list could go on and on. Often in clichés with word repetition, alliteration adds to the aural appeal: "another day, another dollar," "live and let live," "where there's a will there's a way." What mind can resist phrases that *sound* so good? Whatever advice they might be giving us, it *sounds right* simply because of the way it sounds.

In a few clichés, an added appeal comes from an intriguing tension between sound and meaning. These are clichés that combine words of similar sound but opposite meaning. "Make or break" rhymes the ideas of construction and destruction. Opposites are brought together by nearby repeated words in "you win some, you lose some," "take it or leave it," "so near and yet so far." Alliteration combines extremes in "feast or famine," "kill with kindness," "from rags to riches," "through thick and thin." Our minds enjoy the conceptual play of such clichés, in which the sound pulls together what the words' meaning would otherwise push apart. Despite the contrived and illusory way that extremes are united, we still get a satisfying—if subconscious—sense of all-inclusiveness and harmony.

On the following pages, clichés that play upon our ears are presented so as to take advantage of the aural they offer. The point of these is to open our ears to the poetry we speak all the time without hearing it. Just briefly, instead of letting clichés go in one ear and out the other as usual, we'll hold them in our mind and listen to them play.

An Alliterative Alphabet

Not long ago in the literary world, something called found poetry was popular. The theory was that poetry resides in everyday objects and images: The poet has only to collect them. Alliterative clichés certainly qualify as "found poetry." Here they're collected in the most arbitrary way, as an alphabetized list. If you read the list aloud, the natural rhythm and repeated sounds will make you feel like a found poet.

back on the beam
bald as a billiard ball
that's the way the ball bounces
his bark is worse than his bite

Bats in the belfry

beat around the bush
to beat the band

Beat your brains out

has a bee in her bonnet
bear the brunt
hits below the belt
bend over backward
behind your back
the best of a bad lot
has the best of both worlds
bet your bottom dollar

bigger than a breadbox
too big for his britches
bite the bullet

it makes my blood boil
blown to bits
a bolt from the blue
scraping the bottom of the barrel
break the bank
bright-eyed and bushy-tailed
bring home the bacon

Blind as a bat

that's a bunch of baloney
burn your bridges
busy as a beaver
busy as a bee

call it quits
call him on the carpet
catch as catch can
too close for comfort
cool as a cucumber
cool, calm, and collected
the courage of your convictions

the cream of the crop
creature comforts
crystal clear

cutting corners
cutting it close
cut to the quick

a daring departure
another day, another dollar
dead as a doornail
a dead duck
at death's door
give the devil his due
between the devil and the deep blue sea

a dime a dozen
do or die
going down the drain

down in the dumps
drop dead
dry as dust

fair-weather friend
fan the flames of
a fatal flaw
the fat's in the fire
feast or famine
fell at his feet
fell for it
few and far between

Finding fault

that's a fine kettle of fish
first and foremost
fit as a fiddle
other fish to fry

Finding his feet

follow in her footsteps
a fond farewell
the foreseeable future
forgive and forget
out of the frying pan into the fire

gave him as good as he got
gets my goat
has a gift of gab
give him a grilling
give it all you've got
goes against the grain
going great guns
a real gone goose
something's gotta give
green around the gills

had it up to here
cold hands, warm heart
hard-hearted
have a heart
head over heels
a hearty handshake
a heavy heart
go through hell and high water

hides his head in the sand
on his high horse
hit the hay
hit the high points
hits home

A heavy hitter

hold on to your hat
hold your head high
hold your horses
need it like a hole in the head
hot and heavy

jump for joy

kill with kindness
from here to kingdom come
kissing cousins

a labor of love
larger than life
have the last laugh
last but not least
on its last legs
lay down the law

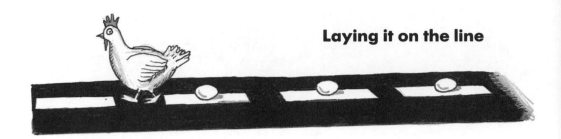

Laying it on the line

lead a dog's life
a new lease on life
leave him in the lurch
let this be a lesson to you
let sleeping dogs lie
lie low
life and limb
the light of my life
if you don't like it, you can lump it
too little too late
live and learn
live and let live
living in the lap of luxury
look before you leap

made her mark
make ends meet
make up your mind
make mountains out of molehills

a meeting of minds
met his match
a method to his madness

Met his maker

a mile a minute
mind over matter
missed it by a mile

put your money where your mouth is
more than meets the eye

The more the merrier

no skin off my nose
now or never

part and parcel
pay the piper
pay a pretty penny
pay the price
like two peas in a pod
pet peeve

picture-perfect
from pillar to post
pinching pennies
pinpoint the problem

pleasantly plump
too pooped to pop

Practice what you preach

pretty as a picture
led down a primrose path
pull your punches
put him through his paces
put him in his place

Proud as a peacock

from rags to riches
raise the roof
rally 'round the flag
a rat race

read him the riot act
all revved up and ready go to
no rhyme or reason
as right as rain
rise up through the ranks

rubs me the wrong way
rules the roost
run into a roadblock

safe and sound
better safe than sorry
saw stars
scratched the surface
send up smoke signals
set the stage for

shape up or ship out
give short shrift to
sure-shooting

sickly sweet
a sight for sore eyes
sink or swim

GEORGE W. SMOOTH

Smooth as silk

a sneaking suspicion
soaked to the skin
spic and span
start from scratch
still going strong
strutting his stuff

swear on a stack of Bibles
don't sweat the small stuff
his sun has set

take to task
it takes two to tango
the talk of the town
stood the test of time

as thick as thieves
through thick and thin

time will tell
on the tip of my tongue
tip-top
tit for tat
fits to a T
toss and turn
wouldn't touch it with a ten-foot pole

Tough turkey

tried and true
turn the tables on
turned the tide

a warm welcome
waste not, want not
weighs her words
well under way
what a way to go
where there's a will there's a way

a word to the wise
work your way up
it works both ways
worm your way out

FINAL FOOD FOR THOUGHT: "DESSERT—THE ICING ON THE CAKE"

Is dessert a cliché? It's predictable: it comes just when we expect it, at the end of the meal. It's delightful: a treat to the taste and often to the eye. It's a social convention, fulfilling a cultural rather than a biological need.

Seeing dessert as a cliché might seem odd, but the point of the comparison is to suggest that clichés aren't only verbal. Or, to put it another way, the roles played in our lives by verbal clichés are played by other conventions as well. Verbal clichés have been presented in this book as serving social, psychological, and cultural purposes. The point to be made now, in closing, is that they're not alone in performing such services.

Our lives are full of conventional responses. Most of us, after going through a phase of adolescent rebellion against conventions, come to respect their value. (The adolescent rebellion is itself a cliché, of course.) We come to appreciate social conventions—like shaking hands at meeting and parting—for the sense of human bonding they give. We come to enjoy the unconscious communal participation of dressing appropriately for the occasion: wearing a skirt or tie to a symphony concert, jeans and sweatshirts to a picnic. Shaking hands, wearing jeans, are behavioral clichés, whose verbal counterparts are, say, "have a good day" or "I wouldn't have missed this for the world."

Whole scenes that we thrive on are clichés. Take the TV sports interview after any big game. Every word and gesture of both winner and loser is utterly predictable.

In religious ritual, too, the repetition of well-known words and gestures gives a sense of communal solidarity. But here other dimensions of community come into play as well. There's the sense of community not only with the people presently participating but also with all the people who over the centuries have spoken exactly these words. And for believers, the ritual language calls attention also to the spiritual dimension, to that unseen reality that must remain a mystery. The very sameness of words said week after week, century after century, carries the words' essential message: "There's a mystery here that we, human words, aren't trying to grasp but want only to point toward and to bow before."

All of us, in our everyday use of clichés, are in a sense believers of this sort. With each cliché that we let out of our mouths, we're bowing before—or at least quickly nodding assent to—the delightful mysteriousness of ordinary life. Without knowing where a cliché comes from, either in our culture's history or in our minds at the moment of uttering, we let it pop out. And there it is, apparently "out of nowhere," expressing our mood or judgment or attitude without any conscious effort on our part.

If this seems to be overstating the case for the value of clichés, try to imagine life without them. The pressure for originality at each moment would be unbearable. And such a contrived constraint wouldn't last long: ritual responses, social conventions, clichés, are necessary to us. They're natural products of our humanness; they're also a chief means by which our humanness is expressed.

Clichés *are* the icing on the cake. (Imagine a cake without icing.) They're the flowers at the center of the table. They're the life of the party, the spice of life, the salt of the earth.

Though they can bore us to death, they can make us die laughing. Though they're nothing new under the sun, they can make our day. Though a dime a dozen, they're as sound as a dollar. Though they won't set the world on fire, they spread like wildfire. Though they're like beating a dead horse, they multiply like rabbits, and the cat never gets their tongue.

They're at the heart of the matter, on sound footing, second nature to us. They fit like a glove, they knock our socks off. They're still kicking, they hold their own, they've stood the test of time, they come just in the nick of time. They're in every nook and cranny, right in our own backyard, the talk of the town. They paint the town red. They jump on the bandwagon. They fill the bill, they work behind the scenes, they come right on cue, they're a million laughs, they're the applause at the end of the show.

INDEX

Every Cliché in the Book

About the Authors

Peggy Rosenthal graduated from Brown University and received her Ph.D. in English from Rutgers University. She is the author of *Words and Values,* which the *Los Angeles Times* called "a valentine for word lovers, a witty and informed study of language." She is married to **George Dardess,** who graduated from Amherst College and also received his Ph.D. in English from Rutgers University. He is chairman of the English department of Allendale Columbia School in Rochester, New York.

The **CRAG** is a free-lance New York–based group of three, C, R, And G, whose work has been produced in a variety of publishing, film, and advertising projects. **Peter LaVigna** is a professional illustrator located in New York City.

Obviously, not *every* cliché is in this book. If your favorite cliché is missing, send it to us on the form below. Maybe we can use it in a sequel. If you wish, include the category you'd put your cliché in.

Cliché: _____

_____

Category: _____

Your Name: _____

Street Address: _____

City, State, Zip Code: _____

Mail to: Peggy Rosenthal and George Dardess

c/o William Morrow and Company, Inc.

105 Madison Avenue

New York, N.Y. 10016